Mary Bridges Canedy Slade

The Children's Hour

Mary Bridges Canedy Slade

The Children's Hour

ISBN/EAN: 9783337372217

Printed in Europe, USA, Canada, Australia, Japan

Cover: Foto ©Thomas Meinert / pixelio.de

More available books at **www.hansebooks.com**

THE CHILDREN'S HOUR.

CONTAINING

Dialogues, Speeches, Motion Songs, Tableaux, Charades,
Blackboard Exercises, Juvenile Comedies,
And other Entertainments.

FOR

PRIMARY SCHOOLS, KINDERGARTENS, AND JUVENILE
HOME ENTERTAINMENTS.

By MRS. MARY B. C. SLADE,
EDITOR OF "GOOD TIMES."

FOR ALL SEASONS AND OCCASIONS.

BOSTON
HENRY A. YOUNG AND COMPANY,
13 BROMFIELD STREET.

CONTENTS.

3

4 CONTENTS.

THE CHILDREN'S HOUR.

TALKING FLOWERS.

[PERSONS. — *Twelve little girls* personating the flowers; a very small child and a larger girl as *mother* and *daughter;* and a group of very little boys and girls as *mosses* and *ferns.*

ARRANGEMENT. — Place the children in a semicircle, having the group for *Mosses* and *Ferns* at one end. Let the two tallest personate *Sunflower* and *Dahlia;* let *Convolvulus* stand by *Dahlia* with her arms twined around her. Arrange the remainder according to height.

DECORATION. — If in the season of flowers, let each have a wreath and bouquet, if possible, of the flower she represents.]

Child (singing: tune, " Nelly Bly.")
Mother dear, mother dear, see the flowers smile !
I wish I could their voices hear — come listen, now, a-while.
Sweet blossoms, dear blossoms, sing, oh, sing to me !
I'll hark to you, I'll list to you, to hear your melody.

Mother (singing).
Hush, my love ! hush, my love ! listen, darling, now !
When the winds the blossoms move, they murmur soft and low.
Sweet blossoms, dear blossoms, sing, oh, sing to me !
I'll hark to you, I'll list to you, to hear your melody.

7

Flowers (singing).
> Gentle child, meek and mild, listening she stands;
> Parted are her rosy lips, and clasped her lily hands.
> " Sweet blossoms, dear blossoms, sing," she says,
>   " to me ! "
> Now hark to us, now list to us, to hear our melody.

Tulip (recites or sings).
> I am a Tulip ; my dress is bright,
> It glitters like gold in the morning light.
> I know I am brilliant, and rare, and gay.
> At first I was proud, until, one day,
> I learned that I was not half so sweet
> As plain, little Mignonette, down by my feet.

Mignonette (replies).
> Beautiful Tulip, the Hand divine
> Made me for sweetness, and you to shine.

Dahlia. I am a Dahlia, with heart of gold;
> The radiant hue of each purple fold
> Of my dress is like velvet to deck a queen.
> I'm the happiest Dahlia that ever was seen!
> But more than my beauty, or pride, or power,
> Love I this gentle Convolvulus flower
> That trustfully grasps my strong, high stem,
> And decks my brow like a diadem.

Convolvulus.
> And I love you, for when I was young,
> With feeble tendrils I faintly clung
> To a Sunflower bold. but she shook me aside ;
> Then you, kind Dahlia, support supplied.

Sunflower.
> I did not mean to be rude that day ;
> I turned to the sun, and you stood in my way.

Sensitive Plant. (*The very smallest child.*)
> I am the little Sensitive-Plant.
> I would like to say more, but — indeed, I can't.

Blue-Eye.
> I am the little Blue-Eye grass ;
> There are few who see me, as on they pass ;

But I can look up with my little blue eye
To the warm, kind sun in the beautiful sky;
And I never am chilled when the cold winds blow,
Because my dear home is so sheltered and low.
Blue-Eye will teach you, in accents mild :
Learn to be humble and lowly, my child.

Violet. I am the Violet, and I dwell
Under the shade of the sweet Heath-Bell.
Early, at dawning, it rings and it rings,
To waken me, ere the redbreast sings.
I am happy, so happy the livelong day,
For I love in my lowly home to stay,
And I know that the sunny days of spring
The love of the children to me will bring.

Gentian.
I am the Gentian, with fringe of blue,
Upward I gaze all the long day through.
I do not know whence the flowers all come,
But it seems to me the blue sky is my home.
When I bloom, the winter draws nigh,
And Asters and Golden-rod wither and die ;
And leaves are falling from vine and tree ; —
Does it make you sad ? It is sad to me.

Columbine.
I am the Columbine, and I keep
Sweet honey-drops in my nectaries deep.
The humming-bird and the busy bee
Know what they find when they fly to me.
I teach this lesson : That free from sin
You keep the cells of the soul within,
That love's sweet honey you may bestow
On all who about you come and go.

Buttercup.
I'm little Buttercup, shining like gold,
With a smile for the young, and a smile for the old.
I grow in the sunshine, and grow in the shade,
I'm the cheeriest flower that ever was made.
When the little ones find me they dance with delight,
As they fill up their aprons with buttercups bright.
"Now, who loves butter?" they shouting begin,
As they hold me up under each lily-white chin.

Sweetbrier.

> I am the Sweetbrier, and I grow
> By the wayside hedge where the children go.
> They search about in my fragrant home,
> And they say, "It is time, for the buds have come."
> But I keep quite still till some gentle child
> Parts the leaves with her fingers mild ;
> Then I send my breath of fragrance out,
> And laugh as I hear the joyous shout :
> "The roses have come! the roses are here!
> I will carry this home to my mother dear!"

Mosses and Ferns (in concert).

> Little Mosses and Ferns are we.
> We dwell in the forest, glad and free ;
> We joyfully drink the gentle rain ;
> We smile when the bright sun shines again ;
> Our fragrant thanks to the setting sun
> We breathe, when each happy day is done.

Flowers, Mosses, and Ferns (singing).

> Little child, an offering
> Of our fragrant love we bring.
> God has made us fair and bright,
> For your pleasure and delight.
> From the garden, field, and wood,
> Sing, oh, sing, the Lord is good!

> Little child, a flower art thou,
> In the dear Lord's garden, now ;
> Gentle dews of heavenly love
> Fall upon you from above.
> Sing with flowers of field and wood,
> Sing, oh, sing, the Lord is good!

Child, Mother, and Flowers (singing).

> Father dear, who sends the flowers
> In the field, the wood, the bowers,
> Joyous notes of sweetest praise
> Unto Thee our voices raise.
> Sing as loving spirits should, —
> Sing, oh, sing, the Lord is good!

MAKING HAY.

(*A Recitation for Summer.*)

THROUGH the meadow-grass, dewy, and tall, and green,
Drives, whirring and whizzing, the mowing-machine,
The horses are prancing, the sharp blades shine,
And the grass lies low in a level line.

To and fro fly the birds, and chipper and chatter,
And seem to be wondering what is the matter;
While Bobolink's wife makes a frightened ado,
As she looks for her nest where the horses went through.

The day grows hot, and the daisies wither;
The funny horse-tedder drives hither and thither,
And scatters and tosses the grain as it goes,
Like a monstrous grasshopper, stubbing his toes.

Then the rake comes on where the tedder has been,
And rakes up and drops out its lines of green;
And the field so fair in the early morn,
When the noontime comes, is all shaven and shorn.

So the wilting grass, and the fading clover,
They all day long pitch over and over;
And men with their forks, as the sun goes down,
Pile the little round heaps, like an Esquimaux town.

While the daylight fades in the golden west,
Let us lie on the odorous hay and rest;
Our couch is as soft as a velvet throne,
And sweet as a breeze from the spice-isles blown.

To-morrow the carts for the hay will come,
And the willing old oxen will carry it home;
And the children shall ride to the barn away,
On the very tip-top of the load of hay.

GOING TO SCHOOL.

(For four Little Ones.)

First Two.

    Little folks, little folks, where are you straying,
      Smiling so happy, and dressed neat and fair?

Second Two.

    Oh! don't you hear what the school-bells are saying?
      " Come to school! come to school!" We're going there.

First Two.

    Little folks, little folks, why don't you gather
      Daisies and buttercups bright by the way?

Second Two.

    Oh! the time hastens, and we would much rather
      Be there in season than loitering stay.

First Two.

    Little folks, little folks, what are you bringing,
      Holding so careful, and keeping so neat?

Second Two.

    These are the books for our lessons and singing.
      Pleasant the tasks, and the tunes bright and sweet.

First Two.

    Little folks, little folks, say, can another
      Join you, and learn all the things that you know?

Second Two.

    Oh, yes; come with us, like sister and brother,
      We shall be glad if to school you will go.

First Two.

    Little folks, little folks, say, will your teachers
      Willingly let us the lessons begin?

Second Two.

    See, here they are, and the smile on their features
      Says, " Dear new scholars, we welcome you in!"

A VERY LITTLE BOY'S SPEECH TO SPEECH-MAKERS.

(*On Examination Day.*)

I SHALL speak very briefly, dear ladies, and dear sirs.
My speech will be chiefly unto the speech-makers :
Mr. Preacher preached a sermon ; I cannot tell you, next,
What was Mr. Preacher's subject, nor Mr. Preacher's text.
But a lady hastened to him, as on the steps he stood,
With, " Oh ! *dear* Mr. Preacher ! your sermon was *so* good !
I haven't heard a sermon, in how long I can't tell,
That pleased me, Mr. Preacher, and suited me so well ! "
Mr. Preacher was delighted, though dignified and grave,
But, such nice sugar-plums of praise, who does not like to have ?
So he thanked the lady kindly, and said that he was glad ;
He hoped to preach acceptably, and he rejoiced he had.
Then asked her *why* his sermon so excellent she thought :
" Oh ! I liked it, Mr. Preacher — *because it was so short !* "

A LITTLE SERMON FOR A LITTLE BOY.

TEXT : "Make it plain." — *Hab.* ii. 2.

I'M but a little fellow to stand up here and preach,
My sermon is to teachers who little children teach :
Habakkuk ii. 2, my subject will contain,   [*it plain.*
" MAKE IT PLAIN," that is my text : *make it plain, make*
Firstly : Small boys and girls don't know very much ;
When you teach a lesson, make it plain to such.
Secondly : I will illustrate just as the preachers do,
By telling you an anecdote, — my hearers, it is true : —
A very little girl in Sunday-school had learned
The story that Lot's wife to a pillar of salt was turned.
Now what a pillar was, this child she did not know,
And in her little mind she thought 'twas a pil*low !*
So she gravely asked one day, (and it was not her fault,)
If Lot's wife, in the resurrection, would rise, *a bag of salt !*
Thirdly : If that child's teacher had shown what pil*lars* were,
Don't you see it had been easy to *make it plain* to her ?
Fourthly, and last, in closing, I'll give my text again :
Habakkuk ii. 2, *Make it plain,* make it plain !

TEMPERANCE ADDRESS.

(For a very young Lecturer.)

I THINK that every mother's son,
And every father's daughter,
Should drink — at least till twenty-one —
Just nothing but cold water.
And after that they might drink tea,
But nothing any stronger.
If all folks would agree with me
They'd live a great deal longer.

TWO LITTLE WELCOMES.

Little Boy (bowing).

I'm going to speak the welcome! all you men and boys,
I'm very glad you've come, but you mustn't make any noise.
They told me to make a bow, and not be afraid of the men!
Who's afraid! I've made it once, now I'll make it again.

> *(Bows and runs off. Little Girl runs on.)*

Girl.

He didn't welcome the ladies! what a funny fellow!
(Points.) Oh! what a pretty bonnet! trimmed with blue and
yellow!
But you mustn't be looking 'round, look right straight at me,
Because I'm going to welcome the ladies, don't you see?
Ladies and girls, you are welcome, just as welcome as can be,
But the men and boys are welcome, just as much and just
the same.
I hope every one, when you go home, will say you're glad
you came.

SAVING AND GAINING.

(Boy's Recitation.)

JOHNNY, running along the road, a horse-shoe chanced to find :
He stopped, and stooped, and turned it o'er, and this came in
his mind :
" I'll pick it up and carry it home, and sell it then," said he.
" '*There's as much in saving as in gaining*,' the Scotchman
said to me."

Johnny found on the lonely shore a vessel high aground ;
The nails, and spikes, and bolts, and bars, lay scattering all
    around ;
" I'll knock them out, and carry them home, and sell them,
    then," said he,
" ' *There's as much in saving as in gaining,*' the Scotchman
    said to me."

The blacksmith bought the shoe, and said, " 'Tis just the size I
    want
To shoe the foot that holds the horse that carries General
    Grant."
When Johnny took the pennies bright, he laughed, and then
    said he,
" ' *There's as much in saving as in gaining,*' the Scotchman
    said to me."

The Scotchman took the heavy spikes, and then I heard him say,
" We'll get the steelyards, Johnny boy, and see how much they
    weigh."
He weighed them well, he paid him well; John danced and
    cried with glee :
" ' *There's as much in saving as in gaining,*' the Scotchman
    said to me."

GOOD-BY, ON EXAMINATION DAY.

Mr. Superintendent,
    My " few remarks " now hear:
    On you we are dependent
    For visits all the year.
To do us good you try. Receive our kind good-by.

    Mr. School-Committee,
    So welcome at our door,
    Now is it not a pity
    We should not see you more?
To come again, please try. Receive our kind good-by.

    Friend, or father, or mother,
    Strange that our schoolroom dear
    Cannot your faces gather
    More than this once a year.
It makes us sadly sigh. Receive our kind good-by.

Scholars and loving teachers,
 A happy time we've passed,
Yet joy lights up your features —
 Vacation's come at last!
For all, to all, say I: Receive our kind good-by.

PLAYING SCHOOL.

[ON EXAMINATION DAY, after all class exercises are finished, let thi
 Dialogue be begun by a little girl, who shall rise from her sea
 The others, as they reply and join, shall remain seated, carrying on
 the conversation briskly.]

First Girl (*to the Guests*). Every one has recited, we've all
 spelled and read ;
 Some, long puzzling answers in numbers have said ;
 We have tried hard to show you the best we could do
 In reading and spelling —
Small Boy (*interrupting*). Arithmetic, too !
F. G. And so, if our friends will listen awhile,
Sm. B. And give, now and then, an encouraging smile, —
F. G. I just want a nice little schoolma'am to be,
Second Boy. Oh ho ! that is jolly ! what fun we shall see !
F. G. But I hope you will all be obedient to me.
Third Boy (*a larger one*). I believe, ma'am, that I can make
 answer for all.
Sm. B. You speak for the big boys, I'll speak for the small.
Fourth Boy. We are all tired of study —
F. G. But this will be play.
Third Boy. Then I'm sure I can promise each one will obey.
Second Girl (*a little one*). I think that it seems rather funny
 and queer,
 For the school-ma'am to sit with her scholars down here.
Third Girl. Oh, please take your place on the platform up
 there,
 Let us see how you look in the teacher's arm-chair.
F. G. I will go to the platform (*goes*), — but I'd rather stand.
Fourth Girl. Oh, yes, that's the way to look round and com-
 mand.
F. G. I must watch for the idlers 'mong so many boys ;
 I must see who is roguish, and who makes a noise.

Fourth Boy. Now, please, ma'am, don't watch us from morning
to night.
Several. You know we have promised to try do right.
Fifth Boy. You must *trust us ;* I always behave when I'm
trusted,
But when I am *watched* all the time, I'm *disgusted!*
Sixth Boy (the smallest). If I were a teacher, I think that
I should
Look less for the bad boys and more for the good.
F. G. Seems to me, little fellow, 'tis not very nice
For a scholar to offer his teacher advice.
You may open your books, study more and talk less,
And learn all you can till I ring for recess. (*Rings bell.*)
First class in Geography, now you may stand, (*they stand,*)
And give the divisions of water and land.
Speak promptly, and let every answer I hear
Be given correctly, distinctly, and clear.
First in Class (hesitatingly). Divisions of land, — divisions of
water ?
I'm sure I can't tell —
Teacher. Well, I'm sure that you ought to.
Next (slowly). Divisions — of — water, — divisions — of —land ?
T. Sit down, sir ! 'Tis plain that you don't understand.
Who *can* give of the water ? — ah ! John, you may try ;
I see that you know, by that gleam of your eye.
John. Straits, channels and sounds, oceans, gulfs, bays and seas,
Lakes, rivers and streams, are the names, ma'am, of these.
T. You are right. Ralph, now tell us about the Great Ocean ;
Is it quiet and still, or forever in motion ?
Give its various names, and then let us know
What is found in the depths of its waters below.
Ralph. Little school-ma'am, 'tis true, though maybe you don't
know it,
Not all have been born, like yourself, a true poet ;
So I think I'll answer that question as I learned it in my
Geography. The Ocean has five parts :
Pacific, Atlantic, Indian, Northern and Southern Oceans.
It is always tumbling and tossing about ; and it has all sorts
of fishes, from the big whale to the little mummy-chog.
T. Very well, Ralph. Our friends seem so pleased, I suppose
There are some who like better to hear you in prose.
Now some countries in Asia —
2

Little Girl.   Give that to me :
There is China; that's where we get most of our tea ;
And Hindostan stretching down into the sea.
T. Europe, Ann.
Ann (*briskly*).   Lapland, Sweden and Norway, and Russia,
   Denmark, Germany, Holland, and Prussia,
   Spain, Italy, Portugal, France, Turkey, and — (*hesitates.*)
Small Boy. Right up in the middle is Tell's Switzerland.
   Europe has splendid cities.
Next Boy.   London, Paris, and Rome.
Next Girl. We've New York, Chicago, and Boston at home.
Next Boy. Asia has mighty rivers, and mountains so high
   That the snow never melts while the summer goes by.
Another Girl. We've the long Mississippi, and Amazon grand.
Next Girl. And the Andes, that stretch the whole length of
      the land.
Another. Diamonds, Africa has, gold and silver so pure.
Boy. California and Black Hills have gold, I am sure.
Teacher. That will do. I would ask you about your own State,
   But I fear you are tired, and I see it is late ;
   If we use all the time it would be a great pity ;
   We should lose the wise speeches from friends and Committee.
   I thank you, my scholars, for being so good.
Small B. You knew we should be so, we *said* that we would.
Teacher. And now to my seat, as a scholar, I'll go,
   And we'll sing the new song we've been learning, you know.

WAYS OF SAYING YES.

CHARACTERS. — *Dr. Twist*, the School Committee. *Miss Belle*, the
   Teacher. *Scholars*, four boys, two girls.
SCENE : *A Schoolroom.* *Miss Belle*, seated at her desk; *Scholars*,
   laughing and talking pleasantly, but not noisily; outside the open
   door, *Dr. Twist*, knocking at the door.

Miss Belle (*opening door*).   Good morning, Dr. Twist. I'm
      sure it is a pity
My school is just dismissed, since you are School Committee !
   Dr. Twist (*entering*).   Never mind, my dear Miss Belle,
      another time will do ;
I like it just as well to make my call on you.

Miss B. Loss to my girls and boys, though I shall be the winner.
You must excuse their noise, so many stay to dinner.
Be seated, Doctor.

Dr. T. Thanks. Have you a pleasant place?

Miss B. Yes; I like the teacher-ranks. I shall stay here all my days.

Dr. T. Perhaps not so, Miss Belle. It may ere long be voted,
You fill this place so well, you ought to be promoted.
How do you find your scholars?

Miss B. Oh, Doctor, they are queer!
They do pronounce so oddly, out in the country here!
For instance, it is funny — you'd think so, too, I guess —
The many different ways they have of *saying Yes.*

Dr. T. Call them, and questions ask; my interest is up.

Miss B. John Jones, — your morning task, have you prepared it?

John J. (*enters, cap in hand, replies, goes out*). *Yup!*

Dr. T. Ha, ha! Have in another; I like the fun. Ha, ha!

Miss B. Peter Bogle, is your mother a little better?

Peter (*enters, replies, retires*). *Yah!*

Dr. T. Ask next yón black-eyed gypsy that stands the window near.

Miss B. Bessie Lee, do you like apples? Would you like to have one?

Bessie L. *Yeah!*

Miss B. I'll call my little Pad, who is never known to miss.
Do you love your books, my lad? Tell me truly.

Pad. Faix, ma'am, *yis!*

Miss B. Come here, you curly-pate. Do you want to be a Mayor,
Or a President so great, or — a School Committee?

Small Boy (*enters, replies very slowly*). *Aer!*

Dr. T. They give us so much fun, they certainly repay us.

Miss B. Kate, is your problem done? Have you the answer?

Kate. *A-us!*

Miss B. Is it not a curious class, a comic recitation?

Dr. T. Yes; though it scarcely wins my *official* approbation.
Will you my pupil be, while I a question ask?
Will you pronounce for me, if I give you a task?

Miss B. Of course, if all the rest have not been fully ample,
I'll do my very best to please with my example.

Dr. T. I came to seek a wife. If now my suit I press,
Will you leave your school for life ? What is your answer ?
Miss B. (*emphatically*).   *Yes!*

[Teachers are strongly desired to use this exercise to correct these
erroneous ways of saying "Yes," found in every school.]

GRANDMOTHER'S BREAKFAST.

[GRANDMOTHER is a very little girl dressed with cap and spectacles, and
white kerchief pinned smoothly down to her belt. *Sally* comes in
and speaks to her, then turns to the *Miller*, who enters in a white
miller's frock, and passes off the stage after he has answered. The
Farmer, with basket of corn, and *Plowman*, with driving-whip, do
the same. At the concert stanza they all come back and stand by
Grandmother's chair.]

Sally.   Grandmother, grandmother, what shall I do
To make a breakfast this morning for you ?
Grandmother.
I'm faint, my Sally, and so you may
Cook something for me, without delay.
I'm hungry, my child ; so hurry and make
Your poor old granny a Johnny-cake.

Sally.   Miller, give me some corn-meal, quick,
For dear old granny is hungry and sick.

Miller.   You must go to the farmer and bring some grain,
And if you will make haste back again,
My windmill the yellow meal shall make,
And granny shall have her Johnny-cake.

Sally.   Farmer, give me some corn, if you will,
For miller to grind in his whirring mill.

Farmer. Go to the plowman, and bid him plow
And harrow the ground, as he knows how ;
The golden kernels to plant I'll take,
And granny shall have her Johnny-cake.

Sally.   Haste, good plowman, harrow and plow ;
           The farmer is waiting for you now.
Plowman.
           Go to the wind, and rain, and sun,
           And tell them 'tis time their task is done.
           The soil for me they must ready make,
           That granny may have her Johnny-cake.

All.   So wind, rain, sunshine mellowed the soil ;
           The plowman hastened to do his toil ;
           The farmer planted the shining grain
           All over the plowed and harrowed plain ;
           The windmill's wing went whirring round ;
           The miller the golden kernels ground ;
           And dear little Sally made haste to make
           The sweet meal into a Johnny-cake.
           And grandmother said —   (SALLY *gives her a cake.*)

Grandmother (*taking the cake*). I'm faint, my dear !
           As soon as you could you brought it here.
Sally.   But, oh dear me ! how many it takes
           To feed poor granny with Johnny-cakes !

IRON — SILVER — GOLD.

THREE RULES.

Question.   What is the Iron Rule ?
Answer.   The rule of savage men :
           If evil is done unto you,
           Evil do thou again.
           That is the *Iron Rule.*

Question.   What is the Silver Rule?
Answer.   The rule of worldly men :
           If good your neighbor does to you,
           Do good to him again.
           That is the *Silver Rule.*

Question. What is the Golden Rule?

Answer. The rule of righteous men :
If evil is done unto you,
Return thou good again.
This is the *Golden Rule.*

ONE LITTLE GIRL.

Two little feet on the entry floor ;
Two little hands at the school-room door ;
Two little lips with a morning kiss ;
One little girl we shall always miss.

Two little feet walk the heavenly mead ;
Two little hands will the angels lead ;
Two little lips sing the new-made song ;
One little girl in the angel throng !

God knoweth best whom to call to go ;
God knoweth best whom to leave below ;
Blest be the name of our Lord, let us say, —
Blest when he giveth, or taketh away !

HURRY ALONG.

(*For four Little Girls.*)

First.   Spring ! spring ! over the mountains,
Why don't you hurry along ?

All. We want you to breathe where the white snow-drift
lingers ;
We want you to untie the brooks with your fingers ;
We want you to wake up the slumbering fountains.

First.   Spring ! spring ! over the mountains,
Why don't you hurry along ?

Second.   Birds ! birds ! far away flying,
Why don't you hurry along ?

All.   We want you to wake us at dawn with your singing ;
We want the air full of your jubilant ringing ;
We want to see bluebird and robin home hying.

Second.   Birds ! birds ! far away flying,
Why don't you hurry along ?

Third.   Flowers ! flowers ! silently sleeping,
Why don't you hurry along ?

All.   We want to see Snowdrop, and Crocus, and Lily,
And beautiful Iris, and Daffy-down-dilly ;
Too long in your underground beds you are keeping.

Third.   Flowers ! flowers ! silently sleeping,
Why don't you hurry along ?

Fourth.   Joy ! joy ! hearing us calling,
Soon they will hurry along !

All.   The Spring will soon set all the brooklets a-flowing,
The birdies to singing, the blossoms a-growing ;
Soon, all o'er the land, her fair feet shall be falling.
Joy ! joy ! hearing us calling,
Soon they will hurry along !

LILIAN'S NAMES.

(Recitation for one or four Little Girls.)

At dewy dawn, at misty morn,
    When o'er the woodlands hilly
Her little feet fly swift and fleet,
    We call her *Meadow-Lily.*

And when she goes where, singing, flows
    The brook's blue water chilly,
And plashes through the wavelet blue,
    We call her *Water-Lily.*

But, ah ! one day, I blush to say,
    When she was wild and willy,
And strove at bay to have her way,
    We called her *Tiger-Lily !*

But what a shame to bear such name,
To be so rude and silly!
She'll try, I'm sure, to be so pure,
We'll call her sweet *Day-Lily.*

THE WALK.

(*For very Little Ones.*)

Mary. SISTER, see this pretty flower;
   We've been walking for an hour,
   Ann and I, and mother too;
   Here, I'll give this one to you.

Nelly. Thank you; 'tis a pretty thing.
   Did you hear the robins sing,
   Sitting in the branches high,
   Soaring to the sunny sky?

Mary. Yes; and more than that we heard,
   Answering the mother-bird,
   Little robins in a nest,
   Chirping as they sank to rest.

Nelly. Mother says some naughty boys,
   If they heard this pretty noise,
   Would the little birdies take,
   Though the mother's heart should break!

Both. Ah! how sad, and wicked, too!
   Such a thing we'll never do!
   We will love each little thing,
   Then sweet birds for us will sing!

IT IS I.

(*For four Little Girls, one acting as Teacher.*)

Teacher. WHEN I hear Kitty on the stair,
   And listening say, "Ah, who comes there?"
   Must Kitty say "*It's me*"?

Kitty. No, no! To be correct I'll try,
   And always answer, "*It is I.*"

Teacher.	When I say, " Who not once, to-day, Has naughty been, at school or play ? " Must Jenny say, " *It's me* "?
Jenny.	No, no ! To be correct I'll try, And always answer, " *It is I.*"
Teacher.	When I say, " Who missed not one word In any lesson I have heard ? " Must Nelly say, " *It's me* "?
Nelly.	No, no ! To be correct I'll try, And always answer, " *It is I.*"
Teacher.	Yes, that is right. Should any tongue Of anybody, old or young, Be heard to say " *It's me* "?
All.	No ! They to be correct should try, And always answer, " *It is I.*"

WHEN ARE WE HAPPIEST?

(Let two very Little Ones sing this to the tune "America.")

Mary.	Is it when birds and flowers Gladden the long, bright hours In sweet spring-time ?
Anna.	No ; spring-time will not stay, And all the flowers of May Fade, and birds fly away To some warm clime.
Mary.	Is it when pretty toys Add to our childish joys, Making us glad ?
Anna.	No ; for if then we find One hand to strife inclined, One heart with thoughts unkind, How soon we're sad !

Mary.	Is it when childhood's days Are spent in wisdom's ways Of pleasantness?
Anna.	Yes; let us sing and say, If we are good each day, Joy shall our onward way Forever bless.

GEOGRAPHICAL CHARADE: RHODE ISLAND.

SYLLABLE 1: *RHODE.* (*Two Travellers meet.*)

First.　　How did you come to town?

Second.　　I *rode* in my coach, my lad.

First.　　For me, the boatman *rowed* me down,
　　　　The *road* he said was so bad.

SYLLABLE 2: *I.* (*Same Characters. One examines the eye
of the other.*)

First.　　I think in your *eye I* something see,
　　　　When your *eye* with my *eye I eye.*

Second.　　*Aye,* if your *eye* you rest on me,
　　　　In my *eye* a mote you'll spy.

SYLLABLE 3: *LAND.* (*Same Characters.*)

　　　　You came by water and I by *land.*
　　　　Did you *land* upon the beach?

First.　　Oh, no; we rowed with a steady hand,
　　　　The nearer *land* to reach.

THE WHOLE: *RHODE ISLAND.* (*A Little Girl rests on a
shield, with the Arms of Rhode Island.　See Webster's
Unabridged Dictionary,* p. 1755.　*She recites.*)

Little Girl.

She 's one of a double trio, New England's daughter sweet;
She sits where the Ocean washes her little, dainty feet.
She's a favorite niece of Uncle Sam, and always has he showed, he
Holds dear, as any sister of hers, his pretty "Little Rhody."
She leans on her Anchor that tells of Hope; Mount Hope is
　　her highest highland;
She's small of stature, but great of soul; do you see she is —

Audience.　　　　　　　　　　　　　　RHODE ISLAND.

ACTING CHARADE: PENNSYLVANIA.

[BROTHER *and* SISTER, *sitting at a table ; the latter writing.*]

Sister. Lend me your knife, if you please ;
This *pen* is so blunt and old.
Brother. You would write with greater ease
With a *pen* of steel or gold.
(*Noise of a hammer is heard outside.*)

Sister. Oh, what a clamor
Will makes with that hammer !
I wish he would learn more quiet habits.
Brother. Let him work ; he is building a *pen* for his rabbits.

(WILL *enters, laughing, and stumbling over the door-sill.*)

Sister. What is the matter? Oh, careless Will !
Will (*rubbing his shins*). I believe you're afraid I have broken
the *s-i-l-l*.
Brother. Of one thing, surely, we cannot complain :
Of elegant manners our Will is not *vain*.

Will. I was laughing at Peter : he wants his mamma.
I said, " Is she lost ? " and he said, "*Yah !*"
It sounded so comical ! ha ! ha ! ha !
When little black Peter said "*Yah ! yah ! yah !* "

RÉSUMÉ.

Brother (*to Sister, emphatically*). You mend the *Pen.*
Sister (*to Will*). The *sill* you broke.
Will (*to Brother*). You say I am not *vain*.
Brother (*to Will*). And when poor Peter cries you "*yah !*"
You laugh us "*yah !*" again.
Sister (*to Audience*). Now who can see the *State* we've made
In geographical Charade ?

(*While the audience or school give the word, let the curtain rise
upon a statue of Penn. See " Higginson's U. S. History."
Or dress a very little boy in complete Quaker dress, and
surround him with thick green branches, as though he were
in a wood.*)

THE COLONY; or, FAR AWAY TO IDAHO.*

[*A Boy*, with knapsack and staff, comes upon the stage. In response to his call, *Soldiers, Carpenters*, etc., come up from the school, in groups of two or more; as the number increases they move on, down the outer aisle, until they make a line quite around the room. All bring with them their tools and implements. This may be used as a recitation, but it is much better with music.]

Boy. I'm bound to raise a colony, to start for Idaho ;
In all this pleasant company, oh, who would like to go?
   Soldiers. You need an escort bold and brave, to guard you
              on your way.
We soldier boys our guns will have, and start this very day.
   All. Hurrah! hurrah! boys, who will go
        Far away to Idaho?

   Lumbermen. We'll bring the axe, we lumbermen, and hew
        the timber down ;
   Carpenters. We carpenters will saw it, then, and build a
        splendid town.
   Farmers. We farmer boys will sow the plain, and reap the
        golden field.
   Millers. We millers all will grind your grain, the meal and
        flour to yield.
   All. Hurrah! hurrah! boys, etc.

   Two Girls. In garments worn and shabby made you soon
        would have to go,
We girls will needles take, and thread, and neatly for you sew.
   Other Girls. And we the snowy flour will take and briskly,
        gaily knead ;
   Others. We'll churn the golden cream, and make sweet but-
        ter for your bread.
   All. Hurrah! hurrah! boys, etc.

   Smiths. Your iron tools will broken be; our anvils we will
        bring,
And blow on blow, with merry glee, shall from our hammers ring.
   Shoemakers. The Rocky Mountains tramping o'er, your
        shoes will be worn out,   [stout.
We shoemakers will make you more, and sew them strong and
   All. Hurrah! hurrah! boys, etc.

---

* Taken, by permission, from Murray's "School Chimes," published by S. Brainard's Sons, Cleveland, Ohio.

Two Girls.   And we, on every Monday morn, will wash your
　　　　　garments clean,
And stretch our lines across the lawn, or o'er the meadows green.
Others.   On Tuesday we will iron them, and make them
　　　　　smooth and nice;
On Wednesday we will stitch and hem, and mend them in a
　　　　　trice.
All.   Hurrah! hurrah! boys, etc.

Soldiers.   When we, the bonny boys in blue, have safely
　　　　　brought you there,
We'll gaily hunt the forest through, and kill the deer and bear.
Builders.   We'll build a sacred temple there, a schoolhouse
　　　　　we will have;
And just beneath the cross so fair, the Stars and Stripes shall
　　　　　wave.
All.   Hurrah! hurrah! boys, etc.

Two Girls.   We girls your stockings warm will knit, the
　　　　　fine soft wool will spin;
And weave you garments strong and fit to do your labor in.
Others.   When you are sick, we'll smooth your brow, and
　　　　　cheer you when you're sad,
And sing you songs, as we know how, to keep your spirits glad.
All.   Hurrah! hurrah! boys, etc.

Minister.   I'll be your minister, to preach;
Doctor.　　　　　　　　　　I'll doctor all your ills.
Teacher.   I'll be your schoolmistress to teach,
Lawyer.　　　　　　　　　And I will make your wills.
Postmaster.   I'll keep the Post-office for you and send your
　　　　　letters well;
Merchant.   And I the spring styles gay and new of calicoes
　　　　　will sell.
All.   Hurrah! hurrah! boys, etc.

Leader.   Now let us clasp the friendly hand, and promise,
　　　　　one and all,
To keep a true, unbroken band, whatever may befall.
So give a cheer, brave company, for Idaho the fair,
And for the splendid Colony I'm bound to carry there.

　　(*All march around the room, on and off the stage and out.*)

"I" OR "HI"?

(Two Boys, dressed as newly arrived Emigrants, meet.)

Pat. Good morning, Johnny Bull ; and it's wishing each other a welcome to Ameriky, that we'll be afther, for sure I see ye've jist come over ! An' where are ye going ?

Johnny B. To (H)Idaho *(pronouncing with the aspirate).*

Pat. To "hide a hoe !" An' what'll ye hide a hoe for ?

Johnny B. I didn't say "'Ide a 'oe." I said *(H)Idaho.*

Pat. Sure an' I'll niver know what ye mane till ye put the spell to it.

Johnny B. Spell it ? I-d-a-h-o — (H)Idaho.

Pat. Is it *Idaho* you mane ?

Johnny B. Yes ; (H)Idaho.

Pat (tossing up his hat, and laughing heartily as they go out). "Yes, Hide-a-hoe !" Well, be off wid ye, and hide a hoe if ye will, and good luck to ye !

LOST STATES AND TERRITORIES.

(A Blackboard Exercise.)

[Write this upon the blackboard. As soon as a scholar sees and finds a name, let him raise a hand and be sent to the board to draw a line under the letters forming the name.]

Is all the ore gone in the mine you delve ?
The columbiad was used in eighteen hundred twelve.
The cut — ah, me ! it smarts like flame.
Louis, I anagram your name.
Birds of the north, carol in a dale ;
Birds of the south, carol in a vale.
Adel a war engaged in with Aden.
Said I, O wait for me, pretty maiden.
Noah reached from the ark, an' sassafras picked he.
Will you go to the Calif, or Niagara to see ?
I knew Yorkshire is in England ; did you ?
I knew Jersey is in the English Channel, too.
Oh, doctor, ill I noise can bear.
Sailors miss our Indian summer air.
In Diana you see a goddess fair.

The Neva dashes a rushing race.
Put a comma in every proper place.
When storm-shaken, tuck your pants in your boots.
Give Mary landaus for riding, her taste it suits.
Once I had a cot ; ah, now I have none !
But oh, I ought never to live alone.
Two towns to connect, I cut a railroad between.
His face was florid at morning when seen.
Thalaba made poet Southey's fame.
Rage or giant despair o'ercame.
I shall do some washing to-night, she said.
Eternal snows cover Mont Blanc's head.
It exasperates me to hear that sound.
Mount Ida houses have galleries around.
Many a color a dolphin shows ere dead.
The common tanager is partly red.
I can teach you to make nice Indian bread.
" Were the tastes of Penn sylvan ? " I asked of Ned.
Morn is dewy ; O mingle with us, he said.
Come, missis, sip pigeon broth made at the fire. ·
Raphael's Virgin I always admire.

GEOGRAPHY.

(For twenty Little Boys.)

First.   You came to see us read and spell,
      And make gymnastic motions ;
    Then, if we sang and counted well,
      We suited all your notions.

Second. If, with eight fingers and two thumbs,
      We showed we'd not neglected
    To add some very little sums,
      'Twas all that you expected.

Third.   You'll be astonished when you've found
      Geography we're learning !
    And that we know the earth is round,
      And on its axis turning.

Fourth.   Round, like this cent? (*Showing one.*)

All.   No; not at all!

Fourth.   Round like this pencil? (*Showing one.*)

All.   No!

Fourth.   But it is round like this round ball,
    And turning round, *just so.*

Fifth.   Upon the earth is lovely land,
    With many a pretty dwelling;
  And 'round the earth, on every hand,
    Blue ocean waves are swelling.

Sixth.   *The ocean!* that's the biggest thing
    There is in all creation!
  And ships sail over it, to bring
    The wealth of every nation.

Seventh.   A gulf or bay is where the sea
    Into the land goes far.
  Mexico Gulf and Hudson's Bay
    My best examples are.

Eighth.   A lake is water where the land
    On every side is found.
  A pond is just a little lake.
    I sail boats on a pond.

Ninth.   A river is a stream that flows
    Through land for miles away;
  The Mississippi southward goes
    Three thousand miles, they say.

Tenth.   Upon the earth, on either side,
    Are continents, — I'll show them: (*Points.*)
  The *Western*, long; the *Eastern*, wide.
    You see how well I know them?

Eleventh.   And where the land, like letter V,
    Goes stretching, in *this* shape,
  Into the ocean or the sea,
    It is a point or cape.

Twelfth. Another thing of capes say I,
 To tell a bigger story :
 That when the cape is very high,
 It is a promontory.

Thirteenth. An island is a piece of land
 With water all around it ;
 So when you walk along the sand
 The waves will always bound it.

Fourteenth. Don't go a thousand miles away
 To find the names of many ;
 The little isles in Boston Bay
 Are just as good as any.

Fifteenth. *Pen-in-su-la* — that's long, I know,
 But then we all can spell it ;
 These folks the meaning may not know,
 So, John, you'd better tell it.

Sixteenth. *Almost an island.* It would be,
 But for this neck of land
 That stretches out across the sea,
 An isle. (*To audience.*) *Do you understand ?*

Seventeenth. And by a funny name we call
 These necks, where'er they are ;
 Isthmus, the name of one and all :
 Here's Suez, there's Panama.

Eighteenth. A *mountain's* a tremendous hill ;
 Some, more than five miles high.
 The Andes see now, if you will,
 Pacific Ocean nigh.

Nineteenth. About the *people* let me tell : —
 In all earth's various places
 The children of one Father dwell,
 Though they're of different races.

Twentieth. The *White* men of our own dear land,
 The *Indian* red and wild,
 The *Brown* men of the desert sand,
 And Afric's *Negro* child.

3

In concert. And now, lest weary you should grow,
We say, *here ends our lesson.*
Of course, from what you've heard, you know
That we are bound to press on,
And learn, each season, more and more
Of every land and nation,
Of every sea and every shore, —
In short, of *all creation.*

[Let every division be shown on the map with a long pointer; show with ball and needle how the earth turns; make motions with hands for *long* and *wide;* make a *V* with your fingers; at *Pen-in-su-la* let all spell in concert. After this, sing the following *Geography Song.*]

GEOGRAPHY SONG.

(Music in " Golden Robin.")

OH, have you heard Geography sung?
For, if you've not, it's on my tongue,
About the earth in air that's hung,
All covered with green little islands.
Oceans, gulfs, and bays and seas,
Channels and straits, sounds if you please,
Great archipelagos, too, and all these
Are covered with green little islands.

All o'er the earth are water and land,
Beneath the ships, or where we stand,
And far beyond the ocean strand
Are thousands of green little islands.
Continents and capes there are,
Isthmus, and then peninsula,
Mountain and valley, and shore stretching far,
And thousands of green little islands.

All o'er the globe great circles are found,
From East to West some stretch around,
Some go from North to Southern bound,
Right over the green little islands.
Great equator, tropics two ;
Latitude lines, longitude, too ;
Cold polar circles, and all these go through
The thousands of green little islands.

Oh, don't you think 'tis pleasant to know
About the sea and land, just so,
And how the lines and circles go
    Right over the green little islands?
Now you hear how we can sing,
This is, to-day, all we can bring ;
Come again soon, and then you shall hear sung
    The names of the green little islands.

GEOGRAPHICAL CHARADE.

(*For two Little Ones.*)

(A LITTLE GIRL *with long, crimped hair enters, tossing her hair and running across the stage, as she recites her couplet.*)

Teacher.   The Charade word has but one syllable.

Little Girl.   If I were a colt, I should toss it, — so, —
      As I cantered along the shore.

Boy (*enters in Sailor's dress*).
      If I were a sailor, across it I'd go,
      And maybe not come home any more.

Both (*coming to the front*).
      'Tis the farthest first of a glorious number,
      And, like an old garret, 'tis *full of lumber.*
      We'll help you by saying it is a State;
      And now for your answer you see us wait.

Little G. (*goes to map*).
      Now, while you are guessing, I'll make it plain,
      For don't you see that I point to —

                    (*All cry*) MAINE !

A WISE DECISION.

(*For Valentine's Day.*)

ON little Annie's valentine,
    With long hair all a-curl,
With gay guitar, and doublet fine,
    A-singing to his girl, —

A love-lorn troubadour is seen.
　Said Annie : " Jamie, say,
Is dat de man will ask to me
　Come live wiv him, some day ? "

Said Jamie, wiser by a year,
　And bent on having fun : —
" Yes, that's his picture, Nannie dear,
　He's just the very one ! "

Soft tremors both the red lips stir.
　She says : " Den, Jamie brovver,
I'll tell him, ' No, I fank you, sir,
　I'd ravver live wiv muvver ! ' "

FOR WASHINGTON'S BIRTHDAY.

SONG. — BIRTHDAY BELLS.

TUNE : " Mount Vernon Bells," (in " *Golden Robin.*")

WHEN the white-sailed ships are going
　Downward to the bay,
Where Potomac's stream is flowing
　On its seaward way,
By Mount Vernon's willows, telling
　Of our hero's grave,
Bell-tones, morn and night, are swelling
　O'er Potomac's wave.

Chorus.　　Tolling ! tolling !
　　　　　With a sad, sweet knell ;
　　　　Ever going by Mount Vernon,
　　　　　Rings the passing bell.

But to-day our Country's Father,
　On the land or sea,
Where thy sons and daughters gather,
　Glad we think of thee !
Joyful songs this day are ringing,
　Day when thou wast born ;

Songs of grateful children, singing
    Of thy birthday morn.
Chorus.   Ringing! ringing!
    While glad echo tells
    Ships that this day pass Mount Vernon
    Ring glad birthday bells!

THAT LITTLE HATCHET.

(*Pantomime.*)

[CHARACTERS. — *Mr. Washington, Mrs. Washington, George, Gardener, Gardener's Boy, Servant, Peddler.*
COSTUMES. — Copy from portraits and figures of early American times.]

SCENE. I. — A parlor. Mr. and Mrs. Washington sit at a table; the former reading, the latter knitting. A knock is at the door. Mrs. Washington turns to the servant, and seems to bid him open the door. He does so; returns; seems to tell her of a peddler at the door. The peddler is seen through the door ajar. He enters; bows very respectfully to both Mr. and Mrs. W. Each politely returns the greeting. Peddler opens his pack; displays various articles. Mrs. W. examines carefully, and selects, after seeming to ask advice or opinion of Mr. W. Mrs. W. takes from her pocket a long, silken purse; finds no money; goes to Mr. W., and asks for some. He takes from his pocket an enormous old-fashioned wallet, gives her some money; she pays the peddler, who closes his pack. George enters, the pack is reopened, and the peddler takes from it *that little hatchet.* George, jumping up and down with delight, seems to beg his mother to buy it for him. She shakes her head, shows the sharp edge of the hatchet, seeming to say that he would cut himself. George seems to declare earnestly that he will be careful; begs his father to buy it, who shakes his head at first, but finally relents, buys it, paying for it from the big wallet. He gives it to George, who thanks him with a polite, old-fashioned bow, bows also to his mother, and then runs out the door. Peddler closes his pack again, bows respectfully, goes out, and the servant closes the door.

SCENE II. — Mr. W. and the gardener stand by a tree. Mr. W. seems to demand "*Who cut that tree?*" Gardener assures him that he did not, and pointing to his boy, declares that he did not. Mr. W. takes the boy by the shoulder; he whimpers, and shakes his head for "No! no!" Mr. W. shakes him. Boy cries. George rushes in, his little hatchet in his hand; falls on his knees, in a comical attitude, one hand pointing to the tree, the other to the hatchet. Then puts one hand on his heart, and seems to be saying, "I cannot tell a lie! I did it with my little hatchet!" Gardener and boy raise their hands as high as possible in admiring astonishment. Mr. W. stretches his arms at arm's length, seeming to say, "Come to my arms!" Mrs. W. and the peddler enter, and lift up their hands in surprise and admiration. *All stand thus for a red-light tableau.*

TWO PORTRAITS.

(*Recitation.*)

Two pictures fair our schoolroom grace : —
    A noble matron one,
With calm, fair brow and placid face, —
    'Tis Martha Washington ;
And Washington, whose strong right hand
    Through dark hours led the way,
Until our glad, united land
    Rejoiced in Freedom's day.

The " Father of his Country," he, —
    His face shall teach our youth
As loyal as their sire to be
    To freedom, love, and truth ;
While maidens learn, as her dear face
    They reverent look upon,
To serve with love, or rule with grace,
    Like Martha Washington.

[When it is possible, have the two portraits as above. Otherwise use "Animated Pictures," as follows.]

Animated Pictures.

Let the curtain be drawn away from the Portraits; two large frames, behind, and, in effect, in which are full-length figures, a very little boy and girl dressed in the Washington costume. Show them first as a tableau; at the second removal of curtain, let them bow to each other, and to the audience, with the formal dignity of Washington's time.

THE WASHINGTONS AT TEA-TABLE.

(*Tableau and Pantomime.*)

MAKE a pretty scene with the same figures used in "*Animated Pictures.*" In front of the stage have an old-fashioned table, set as for tea, with antique silver, china, furniture, &c. A servant, in the Washington livery, opens the door ; Washington conducts Martha Washington to the table with extreme old-time courtesy. The door is closed, the servant takes his place, and Washington bows as in asking a blessing. Hold this position as tableau.

Tableau Second: Mrs. Washington in the act of making tea.

OUR FLAG.

(*For July Fourth, or June Fourteenth, the Anniversary of the Adoption of the Flag.*)

Little Girl (*with a flag*).
> TELL me, who can, about our flag,
> With its red, and white, and blue ;
> How came it to have so many stars,
> And of pretty stripes so few ?

Little Boy.
> The thirteen stripes are for thirteen States,
> That first into union came,
> For each new State we have added a star,
> But have kept the stripes the same.

Another Girl.
> The number has now reached thirty-eight ;
> So here's an example for you :
> Take the " old thirteen " from thirty-eight,
> And how many States are new ?

First Boy (*going to the board*).
> Thirteen from thirty-eight ?   Let's see :
> Well, three from eight leaves five ;
> And one from three leaves two. There'll be,
> Remainder, — twenty-five !

Little Girl.

> And these all reach from east to west,
> On both the ocean shores ;
> And over all this proud flag waves
> And the Bird of Freedom soars !

AUTUMN'S QUEEN.

[For this piece the stage must be decorated with autumn leaves and evergreens. The *Throne* should be elegant with the most brilliant leaves and autumn flowers. The *Chorus* may stand in a semicircular line, partly on one side of the stage, so that they may nearly face the audience and the *Queen* at the same time. The *Solo Voices* come forward as wanted. There must be a *Wand* or *Sceptre* of autumn leaves. The *Queen* has two attendants who lead her on, receive the gifts, present them to the *Queen*, and afterward deposit them upon an altar of leaves and flowers. Each one who enters or retires, salutes the *Queen.*]

Chorus (*sing or recite*).

> THE cheerful, joyous season,
> The Autumn-time is come ;
> With song and shout we welcome
> The golden harvest home.

The QUEEN *enters ; the two attendants sing or say :*

> This fair and lovely maiden,
> With beauty's royal mien,
> Shall, with our treasures laden,
> Be ours and Autumn's Queen.
>
> (*They lead her to the throne.*)

Chorus. The cheerful, joyous, &c.

Enter a group, decked with AUTUMN LEAVES, *bringing a wreath of Autumn leaves for the* QUEEN. *They sing :*

> We come from forests olden,
> Where, strewn upon the ground,
> Lie Autumn leaflets, golden,
> Flung lavishly around.
> A crown of these we're bringing,
> The brightest ever seen,

(*Full Chorus joins while the* QUEEN *is being crowned.*)
To crown thee, while we're singing,
    O lovely Autumn's Queen.

Enter a group with bouquets of AUTUMN FLOWERS.

We come from wild-wood bowers,
    And from the shady dell,
With Autumn's bright-hued flowers,
    The offering to swell.
A sceptre we are twining
    Of flowers and vine-leaves green.

Full Chorus. Receive this sceptre shining ;
    Be ours and Autumn's Queen.

Enter a group with small sheaves of GRAIN *and* CORN.

We come from hillsides, gleaming
    With ripened golden grain,
Whose sunny glow is streaming
    O'er smiling field and plain.
Where gladsome shouts are ringing,
    As merry maidens glean ;

Full Chorus. Our sheaves to thee we're bringing,
    O bounteous Autumn's Queen.

Enter a group with small baskets of FRUIT, *prettily arranged.*

And we the glowing treasure
    Of many a bending tree,
In fullest, freest measure,
    Come offering to thee.
Our fruits with hues are beaming
    That on thy cheek are seen ;

Full Chorus. Their smile like thine is gleaming,
    O radiant Autumn's Queen.

Enter a group with clusters of GRAPES.

And we come, gaily bearing
    The clusters of the vine ;
The purple hues they're wearing
    With brighter tints combine ;
To thee our vine-wealth bringing,
    O maiden so serene ;

Full Chorus. We join our sisters, singing,
    Beloved Autumn's Queen.

The QUEEN *sings.*

O subjects good and loyal,
    Your tributes bright and fair
Shall have my praises royal,
    For goodly gifts they are.
Now, while each heart rejoices,
    Oh, join in sweetest chime,
And lift your tuneful voices
    In praise of Autumn-time.

(*All sing. At the last stanza all join hands and wind off the
stage in some pretty dance, the Queen and attendants following.*)

AUTUMN SONG.*

Sing! sing! sing! the Autumn-time has come!   ·
    With merry song and gleeful shout,
    We weave our dances in and out,
    And wind our lovely Queen about,
As we sing our harvest-home.

Sing! sing! sing! the Autumn-time has come!
    And just as they, in days of yore,
    To Ceres brought their golden store,
    We lay our gifts our Queen before,
As we sing our harvest-home.

Sing! sing! sing! the Autumn-time has come!
    The ripened fruit and bending grain
    Fling golden glow o'er hill and plain,
    And smile the sunshine back again,
As we sing our harvest-home.

Sing! sing! sing! the Autumn-time has come!
    And gaily down the closing year,
    With song, and dance, and shouts of cheer,
    We'll sound thy praises, Queen most dear,
As we sing our harvest-home.

---

* From " The Linnet," by permission of John Church & Co., Cincinnati. Though given here for recitation, it is much prettier with
the music.

A NOVEMBER DAY.

[A Little Child, with golden hair, dressed in gray tarlatan or muslin, ornamented with a few maple leaves, birch leaves, ferns, &c., which she touches as she mentions them. At "*golden* light" she puts her hand to her head. If possible, let her hold a branch of witch-hazel with its yellow blossoms, that bloom in November.]

I COME, a sad November day,
　Gray clad from foot to head;
A few late leaves of yellow birch,
　A few of maple red.

And, should you look, you might descry
　Some wee ferns, hiding low,
Or late Fall dandelions shy,
　Where cold winds cannot blow.

And then, you see, I'm not all gray;
　A little golden light
Shines on a sad November day,
　A promise for the night.

For though gray-clad, in soft gray mist,
　Floating on gray-cloud wing,
I know that I the way prepare
　For brightest days of Spring.

And though witch-hazel's golden flowers
　Are all the blooms I know,
They promise — so do I — the hours
　When sweetest Mayflowers grow.

LA CHANSON DE L'HIVER.

WINTER SONG.

No more the birds, *les oiseaux*, sing;
　The trees, *les arbres*, their leaves have lost;
See snow, *la neige*, o'er everything,
　And feel *la gelée*, or the frost.
L'Hiver, the Winter, now has come,
　Bringing us *Noël*, Christmas-day;
Les ruisseaux, brooks, with ice are dumb,
　And in the snow *les enfants* play.

Décembre, December, *Janvier*,
　　Or January, these are two
Of Winter's months; then *Février*,
　　The short month, and *L'Hiver* is through.
So let the leaves, *les feuilles*, fly;
　　Southward, *au sud*, the birdlings go;
They'll back again come by-and-by,
　　When Spring, *le Printemps*, melts the snow.

THE THREE SIEVES.

Child.　O MOTHER! do hear what a tale I've heard, —
　　　　So bad I can scarce believe!
Mother.　Stop, stop, my child! not a single word,
　　　　Till we sift it through the sieve.

Child.　"The sieve?" The meaning of what you've said
　　　　I certainly do not know.
Mother.　The *Sieve of Truth;* through its *golden* thread
　　　　Are you sure the story will go?

Child.　No, not quite sure; but you must believe —
　　　　It is told all over town!
Mother.　Stop, stop, my child! through another sieve
　　　　Let us sift this matter down.

Child.　"Another sieve?" What can it be?
　　　　You certainly make me laugh!
Mother.　The *silver* sieve, *Is it kind?* Let's see
　　　　If it leaves us grain or chaff.

Child.　No, not quite kind; but cannot I
　　　　Tell my mother the worst or best?
Mother.　Stop, stop! by the *iron* sieve we'll try
　　　　One more, and a final test.

Child.　And what is the iron sieve? full well
　　　　Its test I would like to know.
Mother.　It is this, my child: *Is there need to tell?*
　　　　If not, let the story go.

Child. It is *needless to tell, may not be true,*
   And I'm sure *it is not kind.*
Mother. Then I'd let it go, if I were you,
   Like the chaff before the wind.

CHRISTMAS GIFTS, OR WHAT WE DO AT OUR HOUSE.

(*For four Little Girls.*)

First Girl (to Second).

   WHAT do you do at *your* house,
   When Christmas eve is nigh?

Second Girl.

 We stretch a line at the chimney-side,
 And mother sees it is strongly tied;
 Then hang our stockings, and go to bed;
 And just as soon as our prayer is said
 We wonder and guess, till asleep we fall,
 What Santa Claus has for one and all.
 Then, long before daylight, we haste to pull
 From the line by the chimney our stockings full.
  And that's what we do at our house.
   What do you do at *your* house, (*to Third.*)
   When Christmas eve is nigh?

Third Girl.

 We have in the parlor a Christmas tree,
 And each has his own little mystery
 In hanging upon the branches green
 His gifts for the others, by them unseen.
 Then mother goes in, the candles to light,
 And everything is so gay and bright!
 You ought to be there our joy to see
 When we have our gifts from the Christmas tree!
  And that's what we do at our house.
   What do you do at *your* house, (*to Fourth.*)
   When Christmas eve is nigh?

Fourth Girl.

    We hear in the evening a rousing ring;
    We hurry the door to open fling ;
    And, sure as you live, with his long, white hair,
    And jolly, red face, Santa Claus is there !
    He opens his pack, — we laugh and shout.
    And take the presents he tosses about.
    Then he's off ; but, just after his visit is o'er,
    Uncle John comes in at the other door!
      And that's what we do at our house.
        What do you do at *your* house,   (*to First.*)
        When Christmas eve is nigh?

First Girl.

    We, too, hang stockings; but mother says
    One thing we must do, all Christmas days,
    Just as sure as they come, just as long as we live :
    Some gifts to the poor we must always give.
    So she fills a basket on Christmas eve,
    And tells us just where our gifts to leave.
  Would you know how the best time at Christmas is found?
  Help Santa Claus carry his basket around ;
    For *that's* what we do at our house,
    When Christmas eve is nigh.

WHAT NOT TO DO.

    I CANNOT tell you much to do,
      Because I am so small ;
    But here are things, a very few,
      You must not do at all.

    You little boys must not be cross,
      Nor fret at one another.
    Small girls, you must not make a fuss,
      Nor any such a bother.

    You happy all the day must be,
      And playful as my kitty ;
    If you can't be as good as she,
      I think it is a pity.

IF A BROTHER.

IF a brother meet a brother,
    Fallen very low,
Should a brother leave a brother,
    Farther down to go ?
Every body needs a body,
    Kindly words to say,
When a brother meets a brother
    Falling by the way.

If a brother meet a brother,
    Let him understand
That a brother needs a brother
    With a helping hand.
Every body should a body
    Help as best he may,
When a brother meets a brother
    Falling by the way.

LILIAN RECEIVES, AT NEW YEAR'S.

(*A Temperance Recitation for a Little Girl.*)

SUCH an elegant time, you may believe,
    I shall have on New Year's Day !
I asked my mother could I " receive,"
    And she says I certainly may.

The loveliest cards I shall send to all
    My acquaintance of gentle *boys*,
And when they make me their New Year's call,
    I can show them my Christmas toys.

Kate says she will make me a New Year's cake,
    As white as a bank of snow ;
And I'll ask them *cold water* with me to take ;
    I'm a *Temperance* girl, you know.

And one thing is sure, you may all depend,
    From this first New Year's of mine,
I *never* will give one single friend
    One single drop of wine.

Not I! I think 'twas a dreadful shame, —
  For *I* saw, I *saw* the folly, —
Last year, when Marian's callers came,
  As they said, "*uncommon jolly!*"

So it always shall be at my New Year's
  Exactly as I have stated :
I shall give *cold water*, and then, my dears,
  You will not get *in-tox-i-cat-ed!*

A DREADFUL THING.

IF God had meant that wine should be
  Drink for each son and daughter,
He would have made the streams and sea
  Of wine instead of water.
With wine in every gushing spring!
  Oh, what a dreadful, dreadful thing!

MASSACHUSETTS GIRL'S TEMPERANCE SPEECH.

BURNS says of Nature, (do you know
That in his song he tells us so ?)
    " Her 'prentice han'
    She tried on man,
And then she made the lasses — O ! "

So Massachusetts thinks that when
The women on Committee-men
    Have *tried their hand*,
    Then, in a band, —
God speed the day ! — they'll have the chance
To cast their votes on TEMPERANCE !

WHAT CAN THE REASON BE?

TEMPERANCE.

First Boy. A LITTLE spring by a wayside inn
            Saw travellers every day
            Go, asking for brandy, wine, or gin,
            Ere they journeyed along the way.
            "Oh dear, oh dear!" said the little spring,
            The little spring said she,
            "It is just as strange as anything,
            That they don't come right to me!"

Second Boy. A little brook ran, with merry song,
            Close by the distiller's still;
            And saw the people, coming along,
            Go into that whiskey mill.
            "Oh dear, oh dear!" said the singing brook,
            The singing brook said she,
            "It looks as strange as a thing can look,
            That they don't come right to me!"

Third Boy. A deep, deep well looked up to the sky,
            Near the farmer's cellar low,
            And saw the laborers, passing by,
            To the cider-casks to go.
            "Oh dear, oh dear!" said the deep, deep well,
            The deep, deep well said she,
            "'Tis as strange a thing as tongue can tell,
            That they don't come right to me!"

All.   Three little boys stand up in a row,
            And tell this story true;
            And they cannot tell, for they do not know,
            The reason why. *Do you?*
            But one sure thing say the little boys,
            One *sure, sure* thing say we, —
            The water of well, or brook, or spring,
            Our only drink shall be!

4

SPEECH FOR A FOUR-YEAR-OLD.

I'M a Temperance boy!
See my ribbon blue!
Don't you think it's pretty?
Then you wear one, too!

THE TWO BRIGADES.

WALKING early down the street,
In the morning, you will meet,
Keeping time, with rested feet,
    The tin-pail brigade.
When the twelve of noon rings out,
Round the friendly water-spout
They will dine, those workmen stout, —
    The tin-pail brigade.

There's another army quite, —
Such a shuffling, shambling sight,
In their ragged, wretched plight,
    'Tis the jug brigade.
When the twelve of midnight rings,
These the ones the watchman brings
And within the guardhouse flings ; —
    'Tis the jug brigade.

Now, who wouldn't rather be
These that in the morn I see?
Oh, all honor give will we
    The tin-pail brigade!
But if there is a sight
We'll despise with all our might,
'Tis the stragglers of the night, —
    'Tis the jug brigade.

I DID IT. — NOT, "I DONE IT."

A Little Girl as Teacher.
           If I should ask who won, to-day,
           The game, when you were at croquet?

First Girl.   I should tell you that I won it;
           That I *did* it, — not, " I *done* it."

Teacher.   If I should ask who made the kite
           I saw begun, at home, last night?

First Boy.   I should tell you I begun it;
           That I *did* it, — not, " I *done* it."

Teacher.   If I should ask why Birdie 's hung
           Outside the door, the vines among?

Second Girl. I should say I wished to sun it;
           That I *did* it, — not, " I *done* it."

Teacher.   If I should ask who spun the top
           That went so long and did not stop?

Second Boy. I should tell you that I spun it;
           That I *did* it, — not, " I *done* it."

Teacher.   I'm very glad you're so correct;
           Such vicious terms our speech infect!
           My school I daily try to teach
           To shun each vulgar form of speech;
           This worst one, — always shun it!
           Say, I *did* it, — not, I *done* it.

BREAD-MAKING.

Boy.   How is a loaf of bread made?

Girl.   Into the flour Bess mixes the yeast,
       And she kneads it and kneads it, a half-hour at least;
       Then it rises and rises as light as the snows,
       And into the oven it goes!

Boy. How is the snowy flour made?

Girl. Down to the miller, Dick carries the grain,
And he grinds it and grinds it, again and again;
Then he bolts it and bolts it, as white as the snows,
And into the barrel it goes!

Boy. How is the grain — the wheat made?

Girl. Into the farmer's ploughed wheat-land the seed
He scatters and scatters all over the mead;
It ripens and ripens till yellow it grows,
And into the sheaf it goes!

Both. And so, if farmer, and miller, and Bess
Should loiter and loiter in idleness,
Should play and should play, their work instead,
We should have no grain, no flour, no bread!
We should starve, we should starve in country and city;
And wouldn't that be a pity!

WELCOME TO ALL: ON EXAMINATION DAY.

MR. SUPERINTENDENT!
We give you a cordial welcome!
You are the man who best can tell
If we have worked and studied well;
And I am the boy, with my best bow,
To thank you for your presence now.

Mr. School-Committee!
And *Mrs.* School-Committee!
And *Miss* School-Committee!
We give you a cordial welcome!
We're glad your law has made a rule
You *once a month* shall visit our school.
Ten visits a year! with my best bow
I'll welcome you as I do now.

Friends, and fathers and mothers!
We give you a cordial welcome!

Of course a great many times this year
You have visited us, our school to cheer;
But, more than ever, — with my best bow
I thank you for your presence now.

And now, my fellow-scholars,
I've given our cordial welcome.
Let us try to do our very best,
So that fathers, and mothers, and all the rest,
May say to us, with their best bow,
" We thank you for *your* presence, now."

KATE'S FRENCH LESSON.

(*For two Little Girls.*)

Teacher. KATE, how shall I say, " Come to me "?
Kate. You'll bid me, " Kate, *venez ici.*"
Teacher. And " If you please," how shall I say?
Kate. Pleasantly thus, ma'am, " *S'il vous plait.*"
Teacher. How will you ask me, " How do you do ? "
Kate. I'll say, " *Comment vous portez-vous ?* "
Teacher. What if I pain or sickness had?
Kate. You'd tell me, " *Je suis tres malade.*"
Teacher. If very tired, what should I say?
Kate. You'd sigh, " *Je suis tres fatigué!* "
Teacher. How would you bid " Good-night " to me?
Kate. I'd kiss you, thus, and say " *Bonne nuit.*"

THE TEMPER–AUNT'S (*Temperance?*) AWAKENING.

[SCENE. — The *Aunt* sits at a table, writing; across the room two boys
   and girls are reading from her account-book.]

Aunt (speaking crossly).
      BE still, you children over there!
      You bother me, I do declare !
      With all this long report to write,
      To read at Temperance Club to-night;
      I cannot stand your dreadful noise ;
      Be quiet there, you girls and boys !   (*Writing.*)

> (*Aside.*) I joined the club a week ago,
> Not that *I* needed it — oh, no !
> But just to work for those who do,
> Our city streets and lanes all through.

Sam (looking up from account-book).
> See, Nell ! I find, to my surprise,
> Put down here, " Brandy for mince-pies ! "
> Do you suppose Aunt Ann can think
> 'Tis right to *eat* what we can't *drink?*

Aunt (vexed).
> Sam, put that book down, right away !
> Dear me ! I shan't get through to-day !
> (*Aside.*) I never thought of that, 'tis true :
> But what else for the pies will do ?

Nell (reading).
> Say, Joe, can this be a mistake?
> I find here written, " Wine for cake."
> If wine is what makes cake so good,
> I'm not surprised men drink ; — I would !

Aunt (angry).
> Nell, noisy Nell ! what have you there ?
> You trouble me too much to bear !
> (*Aside.*) Can I be giving them a taste
> For that which ruin brings, and waste ?

Joe.   And I see here a charge for " Wine
> For jelly." So this aunt of mine
> Is not consistent, though she be
> Most eloquent in Temperance plea !

Aunt.   Bring me that book ! When I was young,
> This was the word of every tongue :
> " Children are better seen than heard."
> And I believe it — every word !

Alice.   Well, auntie, don't be cross, but see
> If you will not with us agree :
> Since " Actions louder talk than speech,"
> You'd better practise first, then — preach !

Aunt (rising, laughing).
> You saucy children, though you're right,
> And though you put me in a plight

In cooking, yet I must thank you
For teaching me a thing or two.
And when to-night the people meet,
I'll say, " What's wrong to *drink,* don't *eat!* "

PLAYING RAILROAD.

CHARLIE with Katie, his sister, played, —
The game was " Railroad," — and so he said,
" I'm engine, and I'm conductor, too,"
As he rattled away, " A-choo! A-choo! "
He'd stop or go on, and call and shout,
" All aboard ! " or, " Passengers out ! "
And the names of places he knew about —
" New York ! " " Chicago ! " " Washington Street ! "
But still his passenger kept her seat.
His knowledge of places grew scant and few,
And he certainly didn't know what to do,
So he called out *"Heaven !"* just like a station.
Little Kate sprang up with an exclamation, —
Sweet and joyful, glad and clear, —
" 'Top ! 'top ! *I dess I will det out here !* "

SEVEN.

MOTION SONG. *Tune:* " Alphabet Song."

[1] Strike fingers on desk. | [3] Move uplifted hand from right to left.
[2] Point up. | [4] Clasp hands.

ONE ![1] two ![1] three ![1] four ![1] five ![1] six ![1] seven ![1]
Count the lovely arch of heaven ![2]
Seven colors make the bow,[3]
Brightest, fairest thing I know.[4]
See the rainbow in the heaven ;[2]
One ![1] two ![1] three ![1] four ![1] five ![1] six ![1] seven ![1]

One ![1] two ![1] three ![1] four ![1] five ![1] six ![1] seven ![1]
Nightly go across the heaven[3]
Seven bright stars, the Pleiades,[2]
And the Lord created these.[4]
See the rainbow in the heaven ;[2]
One ![1] two ![1] three ![1] four ![1] five ![1] six ![1] seven ![1]

MORNING, NOON, AND NIGHT.

MOTION SONG. *Tune:* "Nelly Bly."

1 Fold hands. [ed.	8 Hands drop.	15 Turn south.
2 Right hand extend-	9 Stand.	16 Hands fall.
3 Left hand extended.	10 Point east. [rises.	17 Hands move west-
4 Right hand lifted.	11 Right hand slowly	ward.
5 Left hand lifted.	12 Rise higher. [ward.	18 Point to sunset.
6 Fingers twirled.	13 Hand moves west-	19 Shut eyes.
7 Hands clasped.	14 Points to noon sun.	20 Lean heads.

LITTLE ones, little ones, fold each little hand.[1]
What a pleasant sight it is, our kindergarten band!
Right,[2] left,[3] up,[4] up,[5] hands and fingers go,[6]
Now they clasp above the head,[7] and now we drop them — so.[8]

Rise, my child, rise,[9] my child, pointing to the East,[10]
Where the morning sun ascends,[11] when misty night has ceased.
Up,[12] up,[12] on,[13] on,[13] goes the rising sun,[14]
Till we fold our hands,[1] at noon, when rosy morn is done.

Turn to South,[15] turn to South,[15] point again[14] so high,
Where the sun at noonday lights the blue and smiling sky.
Down,[16] down,[16] on,[17] on,[17] sinking to the West,[18]
Till we fold our hands,[1] at eve, as quietly we rest.

Shut your eyes,[19] shut your eyes,[19] lean each little head,[20]
Just as sleepy children do, before they go to bed.
Sweet morn,[10] bright noon,[14] sunset swiftly fly,[19]
Soon we'll watch the evening stars that twinkle in the sky.

LITTLE TRUANT.

RECITATION WITH MOTIONS. (*For one Boy and four Girls.*)

1 Throw up hands in astonishment.	3 Make a low bow.
2 Shake the head in refusal.	4 Stamp the foot.

Little Truant (Boy).

BIRDIE, birdie! up in the apple-tree,
Fly down here in the grass, and play all day with me,

Bird.

   [1] Dear me! how *can* I?   Here's this nest to build,
   Robin's is well-nigh done, and wren's is almost filled.
   [2] No, thank you, little boy; [3] I've something better to do,
   I should be ashamed of myself to play all day with you.

Little Truant.

   Brooklet, brooklet, running along so fast,
   Stop and play with me until the day is past.

Brook.

   [1] Dear me! how *can* I?   Down in the valley low,
   Cowslips and anemones would all be thirsting so!
   [2] No, thank you, little boy; [3] I can't neglect my duty,
   I must hasten to freshen the flowers, and fill the fields with
      beauty.

Little Truant.

   Honey-bee, honey-bee, flying among the flowers,
   Stop your buzzing, and play with me, these long, bright
      summer hours.

Bee.

   Dear me! how *can* I?   What would the poor bees do
   For honey to eat in winter, who play the summer through?
   [2] No, thank you, little boy.   [3] In sweet cells deep and low
   Our winter food is waiting for me; to find it I must go.

Little Truant.

   Little ant, little ant, why do you swiftly run?
   Cease your labor, and play with me till setting of the sun.

Ant.

   [1] Dear me! how *can* I?   In my palace, underground,
   I'm packing in my winter stores, to keep them safe and
      sound.
   [2] No, thank you, little boy.   [3] If idling with you I go,
   I wonder what would become of me next winter, under
      the snow.

Little Truant.

   Bird and brooklet, even the bee and ant;
   When I ask them to stop, all of them say, "I can't!"
   I've the greatest mind to turn about, and run to the school-
      room door,
   And tell my teacher I'll never again play truant any more!
   [4] I will!   Good-by, little bird and bee, little ant, and brook-
      let cool,[3]   [straight to school.[3]
   You needn't tease me to play with you, I m going right

WOMAN'S RIGHTS.

MOTION SONG.   *Tune:* "Tramp, tramp."

1 Motion for sewing.
2 Hands on desk.   [board.
3 Motion for washing on wash-
4 Uplift both hands.
5 Fold hands.
6 Each girl bows to seat-mate.
7 Point with right hand to boys.
8 Motion for driving.
9 Motion for holding plow.

10 Motion for spading.
11 Motion for sowing seed.
12 Boys bow to seat-mate.
13 Boys point to girls.
14 Boys bow to girls. [churning.
15 Hand up and down, as in
16 Mixing bread.
17 Rolling pastry.
18 Girls bow to boys.

Girls (sing).

DRAW your needles in and out,[1] mind what you are all about ;[2]
  Wash your clothes,[3] and hang them on the line to dry ;[4]
[5] I've good news for you, my dear,[6] woman's rights will soon be
      here,
  And the men[7] shall mind the kitchen, by and by !
      Sew,[1] sew,[1] sew,[1] my patient sisters ;
      Good time 's coming, by and by !
[5] I've good news for you, my dear,[6] woman's rights will soon be
      here,
  And the men[7] shall mind the kitchen, by and by !

Boys.

Go along ! gee up ! and whoa ![8] Oh, how dull the oxen go !
  Hold the plow,[9] and spade the earth,[10] and sow the rye.[11]
[5] I've good news for you, my men,[12] woman's rights will come,
      and then
  Pretty girls[13] will do the farming, — let them try ![14]
      Sow,[11] sow,[11] sow,[11] my patient brothers ;[12]
      Good time 's coming,[2] by and by !
[5] I've good news for you, my men,[12] woman's rights will come,
      and then
  Pretty girls[13] will do the farming, — let them try !

Girls.

Round and round the dasher turn,[15] and the golden butter
      churn,
  Knead the bread,[16] and roll the pastry for the pie ;[17]
[6] I've good news for all around,[6] woman's rights are gaining
      ground,

And the time for men [7] to cook is drawing nigh !
  So, so, so,[2] my patient sisters,
   Good time 's coming, by and by !
[5] I've good news for all around,[6] woman's rights are gaining
  ground,
And the time for men [7] to cook is drawing nigh !

Both.

Oh, you silly people all ! [6] [12] Oh, ye children, great and small !
 Don't you think we'd better say, just you and I,[7] [13]
[5] I've good news for all to hear,[6] [12] that, whatever is our sphere,
 Just our very best[5] therein we'll do and try.
   Yes, yes, yes ! my brothers, sisters,[14] [13]
   Good time 's coming, by and by !
[5] I've good news for all to hear,[6] [12] that, whatever is our sphere,
 Just our very best[5] therein we'll do and try !

TEN LITTLE FAIRIES.

[At the closing couplet let all the little hands unclasp, and all the
 fingers move, raised high above the head. Music may be found for
 this in "National School Singer," A. S. Barnes & Co., New York.
 Or use it as a recitation.]

   Do you think there are no fairies ?
   Do you think the Fairy Queen
  On midsummer night nowhere is
   In the moonlight to be seen ?
  Hear the story we are telling :
  Ten with us are always dwelling ;
  Ere our song has ceased its swelling
   You shall see them — by and by.

   In sweet summer, when the air is
   Full of fragrance of the flowers,
  Then our busy, little fairies
   Seek the shady dells and bowers ;
  And they bring us pretty posies,
  Lilies, violets, and roses ;
  Ere our fairy story closes
   You shall see them — by and by.

When the autumn days of glory
  Ripened fruits in clusters fling,
Then the fairies of our story
  Grapes and apples to us bring !
And when soft, white snow is falling,
At the merry children's calling
They will join the gay snow-balling.
  You shall see them — by and by.

That kind works of love and duty
  In the home, and in the school,
Make the only way of beauty,
  Is our fairies' golden rule.
In whatever work their share is,
More and more we hope their care is
To be faithful little fairies.
  You shall see them — by and by.

Softly sound our tuneful numbers,
  For they now are drawing near;   .
Waking up from quiet slumbers,
  Soon our fairies shall appear.
Now each queen shall forward bring hers;
Not a single fairy lingers.
They are — *just our ten white fingers !*
  Don't you see them, dancing by ?

MASONIC.

MOTION SONG.   *Tune:* " Yankee Doodle."

[1] Extend left hand.	[3] Shake hands with seat-mate.
[2] Point up.	[4] Fold hands.

ONE thing there is, about which folks
  Have very funny notions:
They seek to learn, with quiz and jokes,
  The true Masonic motions.

Chorus.   This is one ; [1] and this is one ; [2]
      And here you see another ; [3]
    Things by every Mason done
      To each Masonic brother. [4]

Thus, reaching out the friendly hand,[1]
Or pointing true devotion,[2]
Or greeting each fraternal band,[3]
Is true Masonic motion !
 Chorus. This is one,[1] &c.

And with the hand the heart extends [1]
Across the land or ocean,
With love to God,[2] and to our friends,[3]
With true Masonic motion.[4]
 Chorus. This is one,[1] &c.

So serving God, and helping man,
They ways of sin and woe shun,
And bless the world, as best they can,
With true Masonic motion.
 Chorus. This is one,[1] &c.

BACKWARD AND FORWARD.

(*A Spelling Exercise.*)

[Two scholars stand at the blackboard, one giving the questions, the other the answers; each at the end of his couplet writing the words given in capitals in perpendicular lines. Give the correct spelling at the close, thus : *Flow, Wolf,* etc.]

Q. WHY is a stream or river's FLOW
So frightful when they backward go ?

A. The flow turned backward, you shall see,
A wild and hungry WOLF will be.

Q. Why is a REED that, standing, grows,
Fleetfooted when it backward goes ?

A. The reed turned backward, by my hands,
A swift young DEER before you stands.

Q. Why is the quiet STAR, so bright,
Turned backward, mischievous by night ?

A. Because the star, turned back by me,
Becomes some noisy RATS, you see.

Q. Why does a LIAR, who backward goes,
Oft wet his feet, and have long toes?

A. To wet his feet he cannot fail,
He walks the marsh a long-toed RAIL.

Both. Now spell the words on either hand,
Backward and forward, as they stand.

[Teachers can arrange similar exercises with many geographical names, such as Boston, *Not Sob*, etc.]

WHEN I'M A MAN.

(*For very Little Boys.*)

[These recitations should be accompanied by appropriate actions.]

1st Boy. WHEN I'm a man, a man,
I'll be a farmer, if I can, — *and I can!*
I'll plough the ground, and the seed I'll sow;
I'll reap the grain, and the grass I'll mow;
I'll bind the sheaves, and I'll rake the hay,
And pitch it up on the mow away, —
When I'm a man!

2d Boy. When I'm a man, a man,
I'll be a carpenter, if I can, — *and I can!*
I'll plane like *this*, and I'll hammer *so*,
And *this* is the way the saw shall go.
I'll make bird-houses, and sleds, and boats,
And a ship that shall race every craft that floats, —
When I'm a man!

3d Boy. When I'm a man, a man,
A blacksmith I'll be, if I can, — *and I can!*
Clang! clang! clang! shall my anvil ring;
And *this* is the way the blows I'll swing.
I'll shoe your horse, sir, neat and tight,
Then I'll trot 'round the square to see if it's right,
When I'm a man!

4th Boy. When I'm a man, a man,
A mason I'll be, if I can, — *and I can!*

I'll lay a brick *this* way, and lay one *that* ;
Then take my trowel and smooth them flat.
Great chimneys I'll make. I think I'll be able
To build one as high as the tower of Babel!
When I'm a man!

5th Boy. When I'm a man, a man,
I'll be a shoemaker, if I can, — *and I can!*
I'll sit on a bench, with my last *held so!*
And *in and out* shall my needles go.
I'll sew so strong that my work shall wear
Till nothing is left but my stitches there!
When I'm a man!

6th Boy. When I'm a man, a man,
A printer I'll be, if I can, — *and I can!*
I'll make nice books, and perhaps you'll see
Some of my work in "The Nursery."
I'll have the first reading! Oh, won't it be fun
To read all the stories before they are done !
When I'm a man!

7th Boy. When I'm a man, a man,
A doctor I'll be, if I can, — *and I can!*
My powders and pills shall be nice and sweet,
And you shall have just what you like to eat.
I'll prescribe for you riding, and sailing. and such ;
And, 'bove all things, *you never must study too much!*
When I'm a man!

8th Boy. When I'm a man, a man,
I'll be a minister, if I can, — *and I can!*
And once in a while a sermon I'll make
That can keep little boys and girls awake.
For, oh, dear me! if the ministers knew
How glad we are when they do get through !
When I'm a man!

9th Boy. When I'm a man, a man,
A teacher I'll be, if I can, — *and I can!*
I'll sing to my scholars, fine stories I'll tell,
I'll show them pictures, and, — well, — ah, well,
They shall have some lessons, — I s'pose they ought ;
But, oh, I shall make them so very short!
When I'm a man!

10th Boy. When I'm a man, a man,
      I'll be School Committee, if I can, — *and I can!*
      About once a week I'll go into school
      And say, "Miss Teacher, I've made a rule
      That boys and girls need a great deal of play.
      You may give these children a holiday!"
      When I'm a man!

11th Boy. When I'm a man, a man,
      I'll be President, if I can, — *and I can!*
      My uncles and aunts are a jolly set,
      And I'll have them all in my cabinet!
      I shall live in the White House. I hope you all,
      When you hear I'm elected, will give me a call.
      When I'm a man!

All in concert. When we are men, are men,
      I hope we shall do great things, — and then,
      Whatever we do, this thing we say,
      We'll do our work in the very best way.
      And you shall see, if you know us then,
      We'll be good, and honest, and useful men.
      When we are men!

THE HOUSE THAT JACK BUILT.

(*A Kitchen Comedy.*)

SCENE : *A Kitchen.*

CHARACTERS. — *Dolly, the Milkmaid. Jack, her Lover.*

COSTUMES. — *Dolly* wears a sweeping-cap, has her sleeves rolled up, and her skirts pinned back. *Jack* is dressed smartly as a country lover.

Dolly (sweeping briskly).
      Peeping out at the window, who is it I see?
      Young Jack! silly Jack! coming wooing o' me!
Jack (entering).
      Good-day, pretty Dolly, and how do you do?
Dolly (saucily).
      Not any the better for seeing o' you!
Jack (meekly).
      But I own the house that Jack built.

Dolly (contemptuously).
>   Oh, fie on your house, as still as a mouse,
>   With nothing in it !
>   Your housekeeping — how do you mean to begin it ?

Jack.   There is some malt
>   That lay in the house that Jack built.

Dolly.   Oh, fie on your malt ! no meat and no salt ?
>   Nobody can eat it ;
>   No creature alive — I repeat it.

Jack.   There *was* a rat that ate the malt
>   That lay in the house that Jack built.

Dolly (scornfully).
>   Oh, fie on your rat ! what story is that ?
>   Tell another to match it !
>   You'd better run home and catch it !

Jack (sheepishly).
>   There *was* a cat that caught the rat
>   That ate the malt
>   That lay in the house that Jack built.

Dolly.   Oh, fie on your cat ! does she tease the rat ?
>   Poor thing !   I believe it !
>   You'd better run home and relieve it !

Jack.   I *have* a dog that worried the cat
>   That caught the rat that ate the malt
>   That lay in the house that Jack built.

Dolly.   Oh, fie on your cur !   I'm ashamed of you, sir,
>   Sweet pussy to worry !
>   Go call off your dog in a hurry !

Jack.   There is a cow with a crumpled horn
>   That tossed the dog that worried the cat
>   That killed the rat that ate the malt
>   That lay in the house that Jack built.

Dolly.   Oh, *good* for my cow !   I can seem to see how !
>   Nice Mooley !   I'll pat her !
>   She's pussy's friend, that's what's the matter.

Jack.   Are *you* the maiden all forlorn,
>   That milks the cow with the crumpled horn,
>   That tossed the dog that worried the cat
>   That killed the rat that ate the malt
>   That lay in the house that Jack built ?

5

Dolly (angrily).
> Who says I'm forlorn?
> I deny it with scorn!
> All day I am singing.
> Don't come here, your silly talk bringing!

Jack (offering a kiss).
> Here's a man with *heart* all tattered and torn,
> Would kiss the maiden all forlorn,
> That milked the cow with a crumpled horn,
> That tossed the dog that ——

Dolly (interrupting).
> 'Rout, 'tout, 'tout!   You may just clear out
>> With your house and your malt,
>> Without meat or salt;
>> With your rat and your cat,
>> Your dog and all that!
> With my cow with the crumpled horn,
>> Do you call *me* forlorn?
>> Take your hat and your heart,
>> And begone, sir! Start!
>> Such sauce, sir, as this!
>> To give *me* a kiss!
>> Clear out o' my door (*chasing him with broom*),
> And don't you come here any more!

WHAT DECEMBER SAYS.

(*Christmas Recitation.*)

OPEN your hearts ere I am gone,
  And hear my old, old story;
For I am the month that first looked down
  On the beautiful Babe of glory.
You never must call me lone and drear
  Because no birds are singing;
Open your hearts, and you shall hear
  The song of the angels ringing.

Open your hearts, and hear the feet
  Of the star-led Wise Men, olden;
Bring out *your* treasures of incense sweet;
  Lay down *your* offerings golden.

You say you look, but you see no sight
Of the wonderful Babe I'm telling;
You say they have carried him off, by night,
From Bethlehem's lowly dwelling.

Open your hearts and seek the door
Where the alway poor are staying;
For this is the story, for evermore
The Master's voice is saying:
Inasmuch as ye do it unto them,
The poor, the weak, and the stranger,
Ye do it to Jesus of Bethlehem —
Dear Babe of the star-lit manger!

LAST MONTH.

(*Memorial Recitation.*)

LAST month the sweet June roses bloomed;
I cannot find a flower to-day;
Their fragrance all the air perfumed;
They budded, bloomed, then — passed away.

Last month our little brother walked
In all the paths that now we tread;
With us he sang, and learned, and talked,
And now, oh, must we call him dead?

I do not know why God should make
The flowers we love so quickly die;
I do not know why God should take
That dear, sweet child so soon on high.

But this I know: the year will bring
The sweet June roses back once more.
And this I know: the heavenly Spring
Our dear, lost blossom shall restore.

Oh, little schoolmates, will you try
To love, like him, God's will and word,
Until we find him, by-and-by,
In the fair garden of the Lord?

And will you, like that lovely one,
   Walk softly up the heavenly way?
And learn to say — God's will be done,
   Both when he gives, and takes away?

[After this Recitation, sing the following hymn. Find music in "Song Era," "Triumph," "Joy," or "Linnet," published by Rodt & Sons, Chicago.]

ALONG THE SILENT PATH.

(*For our Little Schoolmate.*)

ALONG the silent path,
   By viewless spirits trod,
Another little traveller hath
   Gone up to dwell with God.

Gone up from human love
   To higher love and care;
From pain below to peace above,
   In mansions, O so fair!

Attune our hearts, O Lord,
   Though they with sorrow swell,
To say this meek, submissive word, —
   Thou doest all things well!

Fit us, O Lord, to go,
   Or fit us here to stay,
That we may walk with Thee below,
   Or up the silent way.

FRENCH DAYS.

[Divide the class; one half asks, the other answers, the questions.]

First.   *Dimanche.* — What day is that, do you know?
Second. *Dimanche* is Sunday, to church we go.
First.   *Lundi.* — Now what is that, can you say?
Second. *Lundi* is Monday, our washing-day.
First.   *Mardi.* — What day is this, who knows?
Second. *Mardi* is Tuesday, to iron the clothes.
First.   *Mercredi.* — Oh, who can tell this one?
Second. *Mercredi* is Wednesday, the week's half done.

First.	*Jeudi.* — Now who has this name found ?
Second.	*Jeudi* is Thursday, alike in sound.
First.	*Vendredi.* — Who can this odd name tell?
Second.	*Vendredi,* Friday, I know it well.
First.	*Samedi.* — Say what is this funny name ?
Second.	*Samedi* and Saturday are the same.
All.	Listen now, teacher, while plain and well
	The names of the days in French we tell :
	Dimanche, Sunday ; *Lundi,* Monday, etc.

PERSUASION.

A STORY FOR PARENTS AND TEACHERS.

To market went Richard and Harry, one day ;
The morning was pleasant and smooth was the way ;
Their donkeys, though laden, were cheery and gay.
" We shall get there in season," I heard the boys say.
But donkeys are obstinate creatures, you know :
If they choose to be brisk they will speedily go ;
But then, if they choose to be stubborn and slow,
Anybody will tell you they'll surely be so.

" Come, Harry," said Richard, " I'm ready, you see ;
But wait till I cut me a stick from the tree ;
My donkey shall feel it ! — my donkey with me,
The first at the market this morning shall be ! "
So saying, he struck him a blow on the head,
And bade him go on ; but the donkey, instead
Fixed firmer his standing as though he had said,
" I shall stay here all day, of your blows I've no dread."

Young Harry then drew from his basket so neat,
And held forth, a sheaf of the tenderest wheat ;
The donkey, in hope he should reach it and eat,
Was soon out of sight, as they ran down the street.
And Harry was full of his glee and his fun ;
He held out the wheat till the journey was done ;
He came to the market, the very first one,
Ere his hamper of cowslips had drooped in the sun.

And this is the lesson I musingly drew ;
Oh, parents and teachers, I'll tell it to you, —
Though simple and plain, I am sure it is true,
And just as I tell you I hope you will do :
Oh, heed then this lesson you see in my verse, —
That *scolding is evil, and driving is worse;*
And *gentle persuasion is better than force.*
For children as well as for donkeys, — *of course!*

TEMPTATION.

One.	CHARMING child, with sunny face,
	Whither are you speeding ?
Another.	To my schoolroom, pleasant place !
	All its duties heeding.

One.	Charming child, how sweet, how clear,
	Happy birds are singing !
Another.	Yes, I know it, but I hear
	Happy school-bells ringing.

One.	Charming child, the day is long
	And the schoolroom dreary.
Another.	No ; we cheer our hearts with song,
	So we're never weary.

One.	Charming child, go there no more,
	Stay for recreation.
Another.	Here's my happy schoolroom door,
	So, good-by, Temptation.

CHOICE OF ZONES.

First.	OH, where in the world would you choose to dwell ?
Second.	Listen a moment, and I will tell.
	Where vines and fruits of the tropics grow ;
	Where flowers of beauty and fragrance blow ;
	Where comes no dread of the snow and wind.
	My home in the *Torrid Zone* I'd find.

First.	Where under the sun would be *your* choice?
Third.	Where Northern Lights should my eye rejoice.

Over the fields of ice and snow,
Swift, in a reindeer sledge I'd go;
And watch blue icebergs floating down,
'Neath the midnight sun of the *Frigid Zone.*

First.	Now tell me, where would *you* like to live?
Fourth.	Oh, me a home in the fair land give,

Where Summer, Autumn, Winter, and Spring
The ceaseless song of the seasons sing.
Where seed-time and harvest go and come;
For the *Temperate Zone* shall be my home.

First. One chooses the cold, and one the heat,
And one the land where they blend and meet.
The Laplander thinks his frozen zone
The happiest land that the sun shines on,
While a voice floats up from tropical bowers,
" The happiest land in the world is ours ! "

All. And is it not well? The Lord hath made
The world in its various zones arrayed.
One girdles the earth with ice and snow,
One decks with radiant wreaths her brow.
From North, and South, and East, and West,
All homes of the earth cry, " *Ours is best!* "

ALPHABET GAME.

[Let twenty-six very little ones stand in a row, each holding in his right hand a card-board letter large enough to be plainly seen in all parts of the room.]

(*All sing to the tune " Yankee Doodle."*)
WE are very little things,
  Standing in our places ;
And now we raise our names high up
  Above our little faces.
Don't you wish that you could learn
  All these pretty letters ?
Don't you wish that you could turn
  To little *Alphabetters ?*

(Let a very small child in the audience say,)
I think if I were you,
I'd show what I could do.

Three little ones step from the line and stand together.
We three will show you that
We spell *c-a-t*, cat.

Three others come out.
Now you can see us spell
*W-e-ll,** well.

Three others. We now, you see, begin
     To make *d-i-n*, din.

Three others. We three will show, with joy,
     We spell *b-o-y*, boy.

Three others. And now we show you, sir,
     We spell *f-u-r*, fur.

First group (recites in concert, holding up the word).
The cat says " mew " and catches mice
My cat is kitty, and she is nice.

Second group (high holding up the word).
A boy is big, can reach *so high!*
A boy will be a man by'n'by.

Third group. Now we will tell you, ding, dong, bell,
     A *boy* put the *cat* down in the well!

Fourth group. It was a sad, dark place for her, —
     It bumped her nose, and wet her *fur.*

Fifth group. She made a *din*, when she went in,
     Then good Jack Stout, he took her out.

A. E. I. O. U. (standing in line, say to the remainder).
We are the little vowels ; if us you do not borrow
You cannot spell a single word, though you stay there till
to-morrow.

---

* When a letter is doubled, the child holds a duplicate letter in his
left hand.

K and S.	Come over, I, — (*I comes*,) — your face we miss;
	Come let us make *k-i-ss*, kiss. (*They all kiss.*)
V and X.	Come E, join us two little specks,
	And help us spell *v-e-x*, vex.
Q and Z.	Come U and I, your place here is
	To show the people how to *quiz*.

*(They all stand in line, holding the letters up to
their eyes like opera glasses.)*

H and P.	Come over, O, and with us stop,
	And pretty soon we'll have a *hop*.

(They join and hop across the stage.)

J and M.	Come A, run over where I am,
	And help me make a dish of *jam*.

(They clasp arms closely.)

G.	I'm all alone, dear brother O ;
	Come over here and make me *go*.
All.	So now we've tried to show to you
	What little things like us can do.
	And if you come again some day,
	We'll try some longer words to say.
	And now we little Alphabetters
	Will sing you all our pretty letters.

"A, B, C, D, E, F, G,
H, I, J, K, L, M, N, O, P;
Q. R, S, and T, U, V,
W, and X, Y, Z.
Now you've heard my a, b, c,
Tell me what you think of me."

(Sing in the familiar tune of "Alphabet Song.")

WHERE TEN BOYS WANT TO LIVE.

First.

UP in a balloon, boys, could you gaily go,
Sailing on o'er torrid plains, or frigid heights of snow,
Over every earthly land beneath the sun and moon,
Which one would you like the best when up in a balloon?

Second.

I'd sail o'er *South America,* and up the Amazon ;
And dwell where wondrous flowers and fruits, grow, tropic trees
    upon.

Third.

And I would go to *Greenland,* the icebergs crash to hear,
And run on snow-shoes o'er the hills to chase the polar bear.

Fourth.

I would descend o'er *Italy,* in mighty Rome to dwell,
And see the homes of famous men whose deeds the poets tell.

Fifth.

Far up in stormy *Labrador,* would be my choice to go,
And try the snow-huts, underground, among the Esquimaux.

Sixth.

Ha ! ha ! what curious countries some people seem to please !
I'd seek some sunny summer isle on purple southern seas.

Seventh.

Sure of your welcome you would be, the natives glad would
    greet you ;
They'd love you so, each wild Fejee ! yes, well enough to
    eat you!

Eighth.

In northern *Norway* don't you think it might be jolly fun
To go and see the strange, long day beneath the midnight sun ?

Ninth.

Yes ; but I'd rather stop an hour in splendid London city ;
To never see its famous Tower, — now that would be a pity.

Tenth.

Now, boys, I've listened to you all, and this is what I say :
I would not change my home at all, — right here I want to stay.

All.

Oh, well, of course just so would we, in real, honest truth.
Our own brave land the best must be for her aspiring youth.
I'm sure we would not change our home, nor leave it very soon,
For any place our eyes might see, though "up in a balloon."
We'll shout "Long live America ! land of the brave and free !"
Where wave its glorious Stars and Stripes, — *that* is the land
    for me !

LITTLE CHILDREN'S CHRISTMAS SONG.

Tune: "A, B, C."

LET us sound a happy chime
For the blessed Christmas-time.
May good-will on earth, and peace,
Newly come and never cease.
Let us sound, &c.

Like the shepherds let us go,
Seeking if these things be so;
Till we find the Christmas child,
Jesus, gentle, meek, and mild.
Like the shepherds, &c.

Glory, sing to God again,
Peace on earth, good-will to men;
Just as once the angels sang,
When the Christmas chorus rang!
Glory, sing, &c.

HE CARETH FOR US.

(*Recitation for Opening of School.*)

Teacher. Read Matt. vi. 28, 29.
School. All over the hill is
The bloom of the lilies.
Their glory and beauty I see.
For them he is caring,
His love they are sharing;
How much more he careth for me!

Teacher. Read Matt. vi. 30.
School. In sunshine or shadow
The beautiful meadow
All clothed with the grasses shall be.
He cares for their growing,
Each tender blade knowing,
How much more he careth for me!

Teacher.   Read Matt. x. 29, 31.
School.   The sparrows are winging,
                 And joyfully singing;
                 If, down from its nest in the tree,
                 One sparrow is falling,
                 He cares for its calling;
                 How much more he careth for me!

Teacher.   Read Ps. cxiv. 9, 10.
School.   The birds and the flowers,
                 How humble their powers;
                 If such little things loveth he,
                 His dear praises singing,
                 My song shall be ringing;
                 How much more he careth for me!

NEUF HEURES MOINS CINQ MINUTES.

[Five Minutes of Nine.]

Child.   *Il est neuf heures, ma chère maman,*
                 Mes livres, je ne puis pas trouver.
                 It's nine o'clock, my mamma dear,
                 I cannot find my books, I say.

                 Où est mon chapeau, chère maman?
                 Where is my hat, my mamma dear?
                 I know that when I'm *à l'école,*
                 At school, "*Vous êtes tard,*" I shall hear.

                 Où sont mes crayons, chère maman?
                 My pencils — oh, where can they be?
Mother.   They're on the table, *sur la table.*
Child.   But some one hid them to plague me.

Mother.   *Ma chère petite,* my darling child,
                 I've often said, *j'ai souvent dit,*
                 Put everything in its own place,
                 And you can find it, then, you see.

Child.   I'm ready, mamma, *je suis prête.*
                 I will remember what you say.
                 Now, mamma, *embrasse moi,* kiss me,
                 And *à l'école* I'll run away.

NATIONAL FLOWERS.

(*Christmas Masque.*)

[CHARACTERS. — *Abbot of Misrule. Rose of York. Rose of Lancas-* · *ter. Rose of York and Lancaster. Thistle. Shamrock. Flower DeLuce.*

COSTUMES. — *Abbot of Misrule* in comical antique dress. *Rose of York*, white; *Rose of Lancaster*, red; *Rose of York and Lancaster*, red and white. The young girls wear white dresses. The *Roses* have red sashes. The *Thistle* of bright plaid. The *Shamrock* of green; and the *Flower DeLuce* of red, white, and blue. Each young lady's head and face are concealed by a very large blossom of the flower she represents; a thin, green tissue drawn tightly over the face and tied around the neck, forms the calyx. Above this the petals are made of tissue paper over wire bent in the proper shape. The flowers are all familiar, and can easily be made with a little ingenuity, care, and taste. Have green leaves of the proper kind, made with tissue paper and wire. In short, make and fasten upon the head an enormous flower and leaves of the kind represented.]

Abbot of Misrule.

> In olden Christmas times they played
> Many a comic masquerade.
> Strange figures showed, who, for their head,
> Wore deer's, or hare's, or goat's instead.
> Quaint, but more pleasing masques have we:
> Upon our stage you now shall see
> England's famed Roses, one, two, three.

Rose of York (enters from R.).

> I bear upon my leafy stalk
> The pure and fair white Rose of York.

Rose of Lancaster (enters from L.).

> To my red blossom turn your eye,
> The Rose of Lancaster am I.

Abbot of Misrule (standing between them).

> Long were the red and white rose worn;
> And long on rival banners borne,
> By hostile armies rent and torn.

> > (*Joins their hands.*)

Till York and Lancaster unite,
And peaceful blend the Red and White.

Rose of York and Lancaster (*enters from* R., *comes between* Y.
        and L., *taking a hand of each*).·
Then England welcomed me to her;
The Rose of York and Lancaster.

Abbot of Misrule.
You see old England's lovely Roses;
And now, before our pageant closes,
Ireland and Scotland show to you
The Thistle and the Shamrock too.

Thistle (*enters* R.).
Where the north winds blow
And the east winds whistle,
On the hills I grow;
I'm the brave Scotch Thistle.

Shamrock (*enters* L.).
You'll find me Ireland's green isle over,
The Shamrock is the sweet white clover;
And Ireland is the Shamrock's lover.

(SHAMROCK *and* THISTLE *stand on either side of the* ROSE
        group.)

Flower DeLuce (*enters* L.).
You'll name my glory at a glance,
For which brave knights have borne their lance;
The purple Flower DeLuce of France.

(FLOWER DELUCE *stands in centre;* SHAMROCK *and*
        THISTLE *take each a hand.*)

Abbot of Misrule.
These lovely blossoms, hand in hand,
Show how the friendly nations stand.
May Christmas joys ne'er with them cease;
Their Rulers serve the Prince of Peace;
While each new Christmas brings again
Its peace on earth, good-will to men!

(*The six young girls representing the Flowers now form for the
    Old-fashioned Virginia Reel, dance the set through, and the*
    CURTAIN FALLS.)

PLAYING CARPENTER.*

MOTION SONG.

¹ Rap with finger-ends on desk.	⁴ Left hand to the left
² Clap once.	⁵ Both hands waive up and down.
³ Right hand toward the right.	⁶ Fold hands.

¹ RAP! ¹ rap! ¹ rap! how the shingles ² clap!
   ³ Here a beam, and ⁴ there a timber,
      ⁵ Then a ⁵ board, so ⁵ long and ⁵ limber;
How the laths shall ² snap! how the hammers ¹ rap!

¹ Nail, boys, ¹ nail! never mind the ⁵ gale!
   ³ Sunny days or windy ⁴ weather,
      ⁵ Cheerful ⁵ labor all ⁵ together;
Soon our house we'll ² nail! briskly ¹ nail, ¹ boys, ¹ nail!

⁶ Rest now, rest; what a cosy nest!
   ³ All well done from floor to gable,
      ⁴ Mimic shelf and kitchen table;
⁶ Now sit down and rest; all have done their best.

ADVICE FROM FIVE, TEN, AND TWELVE.

Five.   You say, "*Me* tell you what to do"?
       Such a wee child as I?
    All that your mamma wants you to,
       And never fret and cry.

    'Tis pretty hard, as I can tell;
       But then, if you obey,
    Your mamma'll say: "Dear, you've done well,"
       And love you every day.

Ten.   Shall I now tell you what I've found
       By living ten years long?
    That quarrels very badly sound —
       Not half so sweet as song.

---

* From "The Robin," published by Root & Sons, Chicago.

That tempers ought to be controlled;
Does any one of you,
No matter if you're very old,
Find this fact to be true?

Twelve. I hear by day, I hear by night,
Mamma and teacher say:
"Be good, my child, in all things right,
And thorough be, alway."

These words oft on my ear do fall,
And these words I must tell:
"Whatever should be done at all
Is worth the doing well."

SPRING WORK.

MOTION SONG.   *Tune:* "Lightly Row."

1 Stand; reach out both hands.
2 Let them fall as on the plow-
handles, bending forward.
3 Throw them out straight before
4 Stand very straight.
5 Turn around.
6 Move the right hand as in sowing seed.

7 Drop the ends of the fingers
briskly on the desk.
8 Wave both hands out.
9 Raise both hands slowly.
10 Be seated.
11 Fold hands.
12 Seat-mates turn face to face.

¹ PLOUGH the land, ² plough the land;
Hold the handles with each hand;
Furrows keep straight and deep,³
⁴ Firm and steady stand.
⁵ Quickly turn around we may,
² Ploughing back the other way;
Plough the land, plough the land —
⁴ Farmers understand.

⁶ Sow the seed, sow the seed,
⁷ Little birds will come and feed;
⁸ Never mind, you will find
Much they leave behind.

⁹ Soon the tender blades will spring,
Just as green as anything ;
    ⁶ Sow the seed, sow the seed,
    ⁴ Pleasant work indeed.

¹⁰ Now we rest, now we rest,
¹¹ After labor that is best ;
    First you know, green will show
    ⁶ Where the grain we sow.
    ⁸ Soon you'll see a welcome sight,
Field so pretty, green, and bright.
    ¹¹ Spring-time through, glad are you
¹² Farmer's work to do ?

HISTORIC PERSONAGES.

[CHARACTERS. — Little Children in appropriate historic costume;
*Queen Elizabeth, Martha Washington, Josephine, Maid of Honor,
Washington, Napoleon, Sir Walter Raleigh.*]

Maid of Honor (introducing ELIZABETH).

    I LEAD before you a lady grand,
    Who long ago ruled a distant land ;
    On her head is a crown, with golden sheen,
    They sometimes called her the Maiden Queen.
    By her stiff, white ruff you will surely guess
    That the Maiden Queen is —
       (*Several voices in the audience.*)
             Good Queen Bess !

MAID OF HONOR *leads in* RALEIGH.

Queen Elizabeth (receiving him).

    And now I call for my trusty knight,
    This noble squire, with his sword so bright ;
    A cloak of velvet he wears, you see, —
    Behold him as once he honored me, —
    As he spreads it down where my foot shall fall, he
    Will surely be known as —
       (*Several voices.*)
             Sir Walter Raleigh !

6

MAID OF HONOR *leads in* NAPOLEON.

Sir Walter (receiving him).
>And I call over the ocean for
>A great and powerful emperor:
>All Europe he sought by his sword to subdue,
>Till he met his defeat at Waterloo.
>I think you must know that you look upon
>The emperor, great ——
>>(*Several voices.*)
>>Napoleon!

MAID OF HONOR *leads in* JOSEPHINE.

Napoleon (receiving her).
>She enters now whom at first I loved,
>And at last from my home and heart removed.
>The fairest, and dearest, and wisest one
>Who graced the court of Napoleon;
>You will know by her calm and gracious mien
>That she is ——
>>(*Several voices.*)
>>The Empress Josephine!

MAID OF HONOR *leads in* WASHINGTON.

Josephine (receiving him).
>And now I take by his honored hand
>The best beloved of your native land, —
>The "First in war and in peace," and then
>The "First in the hearts of his countrymen."
>You now must know that you look upon
>The great and the good ——
>>(*Several voices.*)
>>George Washington!

MAID OF HONOR *leads in* MARTHA WASHINGTON.

Washington (receiving her).
>Come, now, Mount Vernon's mistress fair,
>With gracious manner and kindly air;
>The people know, by the sunny grace
>That shines in her gentle matron-face,
>She is theirs and my beloved one,
>The beautiful ——
>>(*Several voices.*)
>>Martha Washington!

Martha Washington.
>   Oh, dearest, proudest, grandest place,
>   He, noblest of his time and race,
>   Accords so lovingly to me !
>   The Father of his Country, he ;
>   Then, children of his dear, free land,
>   As brave, as true, as loyal stand,
>   Each daughter fair, each worthy son,
>   As is our own George Washington.

Maid of Honor.
>   Now see America, England, France,
>   Join friendly hands for a royal dance.
>   (*Dancing off the stage.*)
>   I go before them to lead the way,
>   And only wait till you all shall say,
>   As swift their feet and the moments fly,
>   To one and all, a kind good-by,
>   (*Several voices.*)
>   Good-by !

AUTUMN EXAMINATION.

(*Recitation.*)

WHEN Spring came, breathing o'er the land,
    Came, calling buds and blossoms sweet,
Our friends, a kindly welcomed band,
    We sang our sweetest songs to greet.
With words of hope and accents kind,
    They strove to cheer us on that day.
Those words, like seed within the mind,
    Sprang up ere Spring had passed away.

The Summer came, and in the woods,
    In lovely dells, on hill-sides green,
The springing plants, the swelling buds,
    The perfect blossoms we have seen.
Within our minds, those seedlings fair, —
    How grew they through each Summer day !
What buds of promise, blossoms rare,
    Bore they, ere Summer passed away !

The Autumn came. the golden grain,
  That gilded all the hill-sides o'er, —
The fruits of every glowing plain,
  Were garnered in for Winter's store.
What wealth of knowledge we have gained
  Our humble voices will not say ;
We lay our sheaves before you now, —
  Sheaves bound ere Autumn passed away.

WHEN FATHER COMES.

SOMETIMES, when father comes, my mother says to me,
" Father is very tired to-night ; don't climb upon his knee."

Then father spreads his arms as wide as they can go,
And takes me up and blesses me, because he loves me so.

I think that's just the way, and just the reason why
That Jesus used these words to say of children such as I :

" Suffer little children to come unto me, and forbid them not,
  For of such is the kingdom of heaven."

LIVE THOU AGAIN, OUR WASHINGTON.

(Recitation and Response. For one Boy and several Girls.)

Boy.   OUR Country's honored Father,
          As in thy name we gather,
          Oh, may thy worthy spirit
          Thy children now inherit !

Girls. In every true and loyal son,
          Live thou again, our Washington !

Boy.   Thou who from tyrants freed us,
          Again inspire and lead us ;
          Nor let thy wisdom fail us,
          Though foes within assail us.

Girls. In every true and loyal son,
          Live thou again, our Washington !

Boy.   As thy great life's laudation
Ascends o'er all the nation,
Our filial spirits reaching,
Renew that life's pure teaching.

Girls.   In every true and loyal son,
Live thou again, our Washington !

Boy.   Till, like thy name's fair whiteness,
In noble, pure uprightness,
All they who now rule o'er us
May shine like thee, before us.

Girls.   In every true and loyal son,
Live thou again, our Washington !

ACTING CHARADE.

MISTAKE.

[To be acted by a class of four little girls, with one older boy as *Director*, and another as *Teacher*.]

Director. OUR Charade is a word in two syllables. It is a thing you all sometimes make. We will now give the

FIRST SYLLABLE.

[The *Teacher* rings a call-bell; the class comes forward. They should walk tiptoe, clasp hands behind them, and caricature class behavior in every comical way.]

Teacher.   Where 's Boston ? tell me if you can.
Your hand is raised ; speak, Mary Ann.

Mary Ann.   Is it on Casco Bay, or perhaps Chesapeake ?
I almost just know, but the name cannot speak.

Teacher (angrily). Mary Ann ! what a lesson is this !
Careless Miss ! thus to answer amiss !
(*To Class.*) Whose hand up, the next shall I see ?
What is Boston ? Sophia, tell me.

Sophia.   I will try not to miss, sir, again.
Is it capital city of — Maine ?

Teacher (angrily).   Sophia! what a lesson is this!
                Careless Miss! thus to answer amiss!
                (*To Class.*)   Some facts in geometry state.
                What's a line and an angle?   Miss Kate.

Kate.   Fishing for trout, in a brook, is an angle.
                A line is the cord you must try not to tangle.

Teacher.   Katie, Kate! what a lesson is this!
                Careless Miss! thus to answer amiss!
                (*To Class.*)   Will no one a good scholar prove?
                Lucy Jane, can you conjugate love?

Lucy Jane.   I'm so bashful, I fear I shall miss it.
                First person — you love — but who is it?

Teacher.   Lucy Jane! what a lesson is this!
                Careless Miss! thus to answer amiss!
                (*To Class.*)   Spell *storm*, and define it, together.

Class.   S-t-a-w-m — bad spell of weather.

Teacher.   You have not recited correctly, — not once.
                Every Miss has missed, and appeared like a dunce.

Director.   We will now act the

SECOND SYLLABLE.

Teacher.   This lesson again you must take.
                Take care, and take pains, for my sake.

Director.   Better scholars of them would you make,
                Something else I am sure they should take.

Teacher.   They deserve that my rod I should break;
                On my own hand their blows I will take.

Director.

THE WHOLE WORD.

[*Teacher* strikes his hand with the rod, while the class begin to cry,
saying —]

Class.   Oh, don't, teacher, don't suffer pain for our sake.
                We are sorry for every silly *mistake*.

Director.   Now, friends, as you saw each *mistake* that they
                made,
                If I do not *mistake* you have guessed our Charade.

SMITH AND JONES.

A TEMPERANCE LESSON.

THEY say Jones is the richest man
　In all the town, and he
Drives by us with his handsome span,
　As jolly as can be.

Old Smith was jolly once, they say,
　And rich; but see him there,
Without a cent to pay his rent, —
　No money anywhere.

Smith bought the whiskey that Jones sold,
　A little, and then more:
So, by-and-by, Jones had Smith's lands,
　And Smith was very poor.

This is the story of the two,
　This lesson here you see:
Don't buy the whiskey that Jones sells,
　Or poor, like Smith, you'll be.

"BIRDS CANNOT COUNT."

A LESSON FOR EGG-COLLECTORS.

First Boy.

　　SIX eggs there were, in the nest of the bird,
　　　Under four brown wings' protection.
　　"Now, 'birds cannot count,'" said John, " I've heard."
　　And so, without saying another word,
　　　He took one for his collection.

Second Boy.

　　Five eggs there were in the sheltered nest,
　　　Karl knew from John's direction.
　　" As 'birds cannot count,'" said Karl, " 'tis best
　　To take one of these to go with the rest
　　　Of the kinds in my collection."

Third Boy.

    Four eggs there were in the nest on the tree.
      Said Dick : "Upon reflection,
    As ' birds cannot count,' I think it will be
    No harm to them, and just right for me,
      To take one for my collection."

Fourth Boy.

    Three eggs there were in that harassed nest ; —
      And I don't know what connection
    There was to the thoughts in the poor birds' breast
    If birds cannot count, — but they left the rest,
      For anybody's collection.

All.   Oh, egg-collectors, don't you suppose
      You might have some slight objection,
    Though you should forget how to count, if those
    Who look at your treasures, should, as they chose,
      Each take one from your collection?

FORTUNE-TELLING.

(A Recitation for Daisy-time. For three Girls, with Daisies.)

May.   DOWN in the daisy field, under the shade,
    May, Carrie, and Kate, daisy-fortunes played.
    Singing, while dropping each floret leaf,
    " *Rich man, poor man, beggar-man, thief,*
    Doctor, lawyer, Indian chief! " *
    This is the way May, Kate, and Carrie
    Learn of the daisies whom they shall marry.

Carrie.   " And what shall we have for our bridal-dress ?
    Daisy white, daisy true, can you guess? "
    Drawing and counting each milk-white ray,
    To see what the last one has to say :
    " *Silks, satins, calico, rags,*" * sing they.
    This is the way May, Carrie, and Kate
    Learn how they shall dress in their bridal state.

Kate.   " On our wedding tour, in what shall we go?
    Tell us, daisy, we long to know ! "

---

    * Repeat slowly, till each daisy-ray is drawn out.

So they pull the florets again apart
To see if the bridal train shall start
In "*coach, chaise, wheelbarrow, cart.*" *
This is the way Kate, Carrie, and May
Learn how they shall ride on their wedding-day.

May.   " Now one word more must the daisies give :
Tell us truly how we shall live."
One by one are the dwellings said,
As they draw the rays from the golden head :
" *Great house, cottage, wood-house, shed.*" *
This is the way the daisies tell
How the brides, Kate, Carrie, and May, shall dwell.

All.   And for fortune-telling, no living man
Can tell one bit better than daisies can !

KINDERGARTEN BIRD–CLASS.

*(One Little Girl asks the questions ; the Class or School gives
the answers. They should be taught to imitate the various
bird-notes correctly and musically.)*

Q. TELL me how Chris-cradle sings,
Birdie sweet, with bright, brown wings.

A. Sing her song, all sing with me ;
Chris, chris, cradle, — Saint Marie.

Q. What is the Whippoorwill's sad song,
Heard in summer, all night long?

A. My poor wife has gone to mill !
Whip poor will ! whip poor will !

Q. Sing me the notes the Whistling Quail
Sounds o'er meadow, hill, and vale.

A. Robert White ! 'twill rain to-night !
More wet, more wet, Bob White ! Bob White !

---

* Repeat slowly, till each daisy-ray is drawn out.

Q. What does Robin-redbreast say,
Waking up at dawn of day?

A. Cheer up! cheer up! cheer! cheer! cheer!
Ripe, ripe cherries! quick! quick! here!

Q. What does the saucy Kill-deer cry,
Chasing the hawk across the sky?

A. He drives the hawk as he flies in fear,
And he sings, Kill-deer! kill-deer! kill-deer!

Q. What is the brave little Snowbird's sound,
When snow lies deep on the frozen ground?

A. Naught for the cold and wind cares he:
Chick-a-chick-a-dee-dee, dee, dee, dee!

Q. What do the little birds do at night,
When the sun in the west sinks out of sight?

A. Heads under their wings they go to sleep,
And the last they say is, Peep — peep — peep!

(*All put the right arm up over the eyes, and say the "peep,
peep," slowly and sleepily.*)

AUGUST.

(*Recitation for a Little Girl personating* AUGUST.)

I COME! I come! and the waving field
Its wealth of golden grain shall yield.
In the hush and heat of glowing noon,
The insects' hum is the only tune;
For the merriest birds forget to sing,
And sit in the shade with drooping wing.

But see! how the purpling grapes hang high,
And ripen beneath my sunny sky!
And see! how the fruits of the bending tree
Turn blushing and rosy cheeks to me!
And soon shall your garners be over-full
With gifts from the August bountiful.

WHEN DO YOU SING?

(*For very Little Ones.*)

Boy. LITTLE bird, so gayly winging,
    Say, when is your hour of singing?

Girl. When the sun smiles up the heaven,
    Till he calmly sinks at even.

Sec. B. Little brook, with music ringing,
    Say, when is your hour of singing?

Sec. G. When the waves at sunrise glisten,
    Till the stars look down and listen.

First B. Little hearts, with gladness springing,
    Say, when is your hour of singing?

All. From life's morn, when song is given,
    Till we sing our songs in heaven.

BIRD SONGS.

(*For June.*)

WHEN the rosy light of day
 O'er the hillside flushes,
Then begins the roundelay
 Of the happy Thrushes.
Soon as misty shades of night
 From the valleys clear up,
Robin sings with all his might,
 Cheer up! cheer up! cheer up!

Chris-chris-cradle's silver song
 Rings among the sedges;
Chipping Sparrows cheep, along
 All the dewy hedges.
Phebe, by the tinkling rills,
 Sings with Wrens and Swallows;
Merry Bob-o'-Lincoln trills
 O'er the grassy hollows.

Mellow lays, so clear and rare,
    Sweet Chewink is ringing.
From his castle in the air
    Oriole is singing.
Down the hill the Cuckoo calls,
    And the Ringdove's cooing,
Soft as summer zephyr falls,
    In its notes of wooing.

From the wood the Quail is heard
    Prating of the weather;
While the gleeful Mockingbird
    Sings all songs together.
Lovely songsters of the air,
    Sound your notes of gladness,
Drive away our thoughts of care,
    Sing away our sadness.

WE'LL TRY.

(*Autumn Recitation.*)

Little Girl.   WHEN Spring came, calling to the Flowers,
    "Come forth, there's work to do !
The blossoming for Summer hours,
    And Autumn's ripening, too;"
Did any little tender plant
    Shrink down beneath the soil?
Did any floweret sigh, "I can't !"
    When called to Summer toil?

Several.   Ah, no !   They said : "We'll try, we'll try,
    We'll see what we can do ;
We'll bud and bloom, nor ever sigh
    The livelong Spring-time through !"

Little Girl.   In Spring-time, when before us lay
    The work for Summer hours,
There came, to cheer us on our way,
    As sunshine cheers, the Flowers,

A kindly and a welcome band
　Of friends and parents dear;
Oh, could we shrink from pleasant work
　When these were smiling near?

Several.　Ah, no! We said : " We'll try, we'll try,
　　　We'll see what we can do;
　　We'll patient toil, nor ever sigh,
　　　The livelong Summer through!"

Little Girl. The Flowers that budded in the Spring
　　　Have blossomed in the sun,
　　And Autumn's garnered Sheaves may sing,
　　　" The season's work is done!" —
　　Kind friends, our season, too, is done,
　　　Our Summer's work is o'er;
　　We would that, for each sheaf we've won,
　　　We had a hundred more!

Several.　Cheered by your love, we'll try, we'll try,
　　　To see what we can do.
　　Begin anew, and never sigh,
　　　Autumn nor Winter through.

AT THE CHRISTMAS-TREE.

Some love the oak-tree, stout and tall;
　The willow, bending long;
The elm, whose branches graceful fall;
　The pine, with sweet, sad song;
The cherry-tree, whose petals white
　Fall soft in summer snow;
The apple-tree, with blossoms bright,
　And fruit of golden glow.

But this strange tree, our favorite
　Through one glad hour shall be;
For love's dear blossoms cover it —
　It is our Christmas-Tree!

Around it as we stand to-night,
　We joyfully declare,
Some lovely fruit, or blossom bright,
　For each its boughs shall bear.

His rain and sun our Father lends
　To deck the forest trees;
His love in human hearts he sends
　To bring such bloom as these.
So while we thank the hands of love
　That Christmas gifts bestow,
We'll praise the tender Heart above,
　Whence all our blessings flow.

ALL THE SEASONS.

(For four Speakers.)

First. SPRING-TIME is coming! search for the May-flowers!
　Brush off the brown leaves, the darlings are here!
Joy of the Spring hours, picking the May-flowers!
　Kiss the Spring beauties, the babes of the year!

Second.
　Summer is coming! gather the clovers;
　Here are the blossoms, all crimson and white.
All round we find them! pick them and bind them;
　Place on our foreheads the garlands so bright.

Third.
　Autumn is coming! high hang the apples;
　Reach to the branches, so rosy and fair.
Give them a shaking, ripest fruit taking;
　Here is a plenty, with you we will share.

Fourth.
　Winter is coming! snow-flakes are flying;
　See how they gather all over the ground!
Thickly the snow falls, make up the snowballs,
　Keep them a-tossing around and around.

All. Spring, Summer, Autumn, Winter are flying;
　Each has a beauty unlike all the rest.
This is the reason why every season
　Always, in passing, seems gayest and best.

MON JARDIN : MY GARDEN.

(Recitation for Juvenile French Scholars.)

Le Printemps, Spring, no more is here ;
And I, *ma chère mère*, mother dear,
My garden, *mon jardin*, enjoy ;
The flowers, *les fleurs*, my time employ.
I'll have, now Summer comes, — *l'Été*, —
Les roses, the roses, every day ;
Daisies I'll have, — *les marguerites*, —
And violets, *les violettes*, so sweet.
And heliotrope, in French the same ;
With *hélianthe*, the grander name
For sunflower ; and these yellow-heads
Shall nod above my garden-beds.
To keep *mon jardin*, I will take
My hoe, my shovel, and my rake,
Ma houe, ma pelle, et mon râteau ;
And good results my work shall show.
No *herbes sauvages* (those words mean weeds)
Shall check the growth of my flower-seeds ;
La pluie, the rain, my plants shall shower ;
The sun, *le soleil*, kiss each flower ;
La rosée — that's the gentle dew —
Refresh them when the day is through ;
And so *mon jardin* every day
Shall with *les fleurs* my care repay.

CHACUN À SON GOÛT : TASTES DIFFER.

| 1 The monkeys. | 3 The rabbits. |
| 2 A walrus. | 4 The Guinea pigs. |

Eddie.

I WENT out with father, a few days ago,
When all my examples were done ;
And I saw *le lion* and *le tigre* at a show ;
Les singes,[1] *l'éléphant*, and *le rhinocéros ;*
Un cheval marin ;[2] and I'm sure I don't know
How a fellow could have greater fun.

Emma.

I went, too.   And, Eddie, it is a surprise
That you could like monkeys as well
As *un perroquet*, who talked very wise
(That means parrot) ; *les lapins*,³ with little pink eyes,
And *les cochons d'Inde*,⁴ of very small size,
Un paon (peacock), and *gazelle.*

Eddie.

I like what I like ; and the same, Em, with you
We will not dispute ; for *chacun à son goût*
Is a proverb, which means, " every one as he pleases,"
As long as with *his* likes he no one else teases.

THE TEMPERANCE SHEEP.*

Say, young folks, will you hear my story ?
  It was truly told to me :
The temperance scheme of John, the farmer,
  In the land of Genesee :
He told his boys, one fine Spring morning,
  If they all the pledge would keep,
He'd give each one, to help him remember,
  Such a likely year-old sheep !

Chorus. — The boys all said, " Oh, yes ! " and John the
      farmer cried,
    " Oh ho ! I've temperance sheep a plenty ;
      every one shall be supplied."

Now I must own that John, the farmer,
  Was a trifle apt to take
A " wee bit drap " from his decanter,
  Only for " the stomach's sake."
But temperance pledge, a cure for folly,
  All the young, he said, should keep ;
And so he felt — oh ! " uncommon jolly,"
  As he gave away his sheep !

          Chorus. — The boys all said, &c.

---

* From " Musical Fountain," published by Root & Sons, Chicago.

Well pleased, I ween, was John, the farmer,
　　Until Jack, a sly young elf,
Said, " Say, now, father, wouldn't you better
　　Take a year-old sheep yourself? "
Down fell the eyes of John, the farmer,
　　And he kept them down until
He signed the pledge that lay on the table,
　　As he said, " My boys, I will ! "

　　　　Chorus. — The boys all cried, &c.

WINTRY STORMS.

MOTION SONG.

1 Let the raised hands gently fall, with waving motion.
2 Fold hands.　　　[motion.
3 Raised hands fall with quick
4 Raised hands wave right and left.
5 Raised hands fall with quick motion, right and left.

THIS is the way the snow comes down,
　　¹ Softly, softly falling.
So He giveth the snow-like wool,
² Fair and white and beautiful.
This is the way the snow comes down,
　　¹ Softly, softly falling.

This is the way the rain comes down,³
　　Swiftly, swiftly falling.
So He sendeth the welcome rain ²
Over field and hill and plain.
This is the way the rain comes down,³
　　Swiftly, swiftly falling.

This is the way the frost comes down,⁴
　　Widely, widely falling.
So it spreadeth, all through the night,
Shining cold and pure and white.²
This is the way the frost comes down,⁴
　　Widely, widely falling.

7

This is the way the hail comes down,[5]
　Loudly, loudly falling ;
So it flieth beneath the cloud,[2]
　Swift and strong, and wild and loud.
This is the way the hail comes down,[5]
　Loudly, loudly falling.

Wonderful, Lord, are all thy works,[2]
　Wheresoever falling ;
All their various voices raise,
　Speaking forth their Maker's praise.
Wonderful, Lord, are all thy works,
　Wheresoever falling.

INDEPENDENCE DAY.[*]

(*Recitation and Song.*)

Recitation.　THE year is full of days that mark
　　　　Our Country's growing fame,
　　　Since, sailing o'er the waters dark,
　　　　Our fathers hither came.
　　　O'er fields of peace or fields of war,
　　　　We look away, away,
　　　And gaze through gath'ring years, afar,
　　　　On Freedom's natal day.

Song.　　Ring a merry peal of bells,
　　　　While the roar of cannon swells ;
　　　Fling the banners to the morning breeze,
　　　　Float the streamers o'er the land and seas ;
　　　Spread the Red, and White, and Blue,
　　　　All the happy nation through.
　　　Shouting, with a voice of glee, boys,
　　　　A song for Independence Day.

Recitation.　Our Country's annals gleam and burn,
　　　　That tell her storied age.
　　　To-day, with loving hand we turn
　　　　Her noblest, early page.

---

[*] This song, with the music, may be found in the "Golden Robin," published by Oliver Ditson, Boston.

No day in all our nation's life
 So grand as this shall be;
When, facing death, and pain, and strife,
 They wrote: "All men are free!"

Song. Ring a merry peal of bells, &c.

Recitation. And though, with grand, heroic names,
 Our hearts are full to-day,
Not one a higher tribute claims
 Than those who led the way.
We honor that devoted band
 Of tried and truest worth;
Charles Carroll, of the Southern land,
 John Hancock, of the North.

Song. Ring a merry peal of bells, &c.

Recitation. Bring garlands of the fairest flowers;
 Wreathe high the arches green.
Let gladness fill the flying hours,
 And glory gild the scene.
Let all the air resound with mirth,
 And songs of happy cheer;
And crown the nation's day of birth,
 The best of all the year.

Song. Ring a merry peal of bells, &c.

MARCH.

(*A Marching Recitation.*)

The stormy March has come again, —
 March! March! March!
And rattling down the window pane, —
 March! March! March!
Come rushing torrents of the rain, —
 March! March! March!
But o'er my head my hat I swing,
And shout hurrah! like anything!
Because it is the first of Spring, —
 March! March! March!

MISTS.

MOTION SONG.

1 Hands slowly rise.
2 Hands and fingers shake.
3 Hands slowly fall.
4 Fingers patter on the desk.
5 Hands move slowly to and
    fro.

6 Bend the head till lips touch
    the desk.
7 Hands on desk.
8 Raise right hand.
9 Raise left hand.
10 Clasp hands.

THIS is the way the mist goes up,[1]
From grass and leaf, and violet cup,[1]
And softly, gently, rising high,[1]
Goes hurrying o'er the bright blue sky.[2]
    Mist,[3] mist,[3] beautiful mist![3]
This is the way the mist goes up,[1]
From grass and leaf, and violet cup.[1]

This is the way it whirls around,[2]
And turns to drops that fall to the ground;[4]
And this is the way the rushing rain[4]
Comes pattering on the flowers again.[4]
    Rain, rain, beautiful rain![1]
This is the way it whirls around,[2]
And turns to drops that fall to the ground.[3]

This is the way the streams and rills[5]
Go speeding on o'er meadows and hills;[5]
And this is the way, by flowery brink,[6]
We merrily stoop, and gaily drink.[6]
    Stream, stream, beautiful stream![7]
This is the way the streams and rills[5]
Go speeding on o'er meadows and hills.[5]

This is the way we raise our hand,[8]
And pledge ourselves a temperance band.[9]
While showers come down,[4] and rivers run,[5]
Intemperance we will surely shun!
    Pledge, pledge, beautiful pledge![10]
This is the way we raise our hand,
And pledge ourselves a temperance band.[7]

THE PASSING SEASONS.*

(*A Cantatina.*)

[Select eighteen children to personate and sing the first eighteen verses, as follows: — *Old Year*, 1st verse; *New Year*, 2d verse; *Spring*, 3d; *March*, 4th; *April*, 5th; *May*, 6th; *Summer*, 7th; *June*, 8th; *July*, 9th; *August*, 10th; *Autumn*, 11th; *September*, 12th; *October*, 13th; *November*, 14th; *Winter*, 15th; *December*, 16th; *January*, 17th; *February*, 18th. All sing the 19th and 20th verses, and also the part marked by the months composing the different seasons, which comes after 4th, 8th, 12th, 16th, and 20th verses.

As a school exercise this may be sung by having the eighteen children, in turn, rise in their places, and sing their verses, the school remaining seated until the 19th verse, then all rise to end with. To give it more elaborately, all but the eighteen could be seated back on a stage (or, as the piece is not very long, they could stand, if there is not room for seats).

There should be a raised seat for a throne in the centre, with *Old Year* in it at the beginning — the other seventeen being out of sight. But they come on, one by one, promptly, in their turn, so that as quick as one is through the next begins.

Old Year, *New Year*, and *Winter* should be boys, but the other fifteen should be girls. *Old Year* hands his sceptre to *New Year* as he leaves the throne. *New Year* remains on the throne during the piece. *Old Year* should pass out of sight after leaving the throne, but may return to the chorus after divesting himself of his aged appearance (if he is in costume).

After each solo (which should be sung well in front), let the singer pass to such a position that at the end *Spring* and *Summer* and their months will be on one side of the throne, and *Autumn* and *Winter* with their months on the other. They may be a little in front of the throne, and two deep, if there is not room for a single line.

The stage may be decorated with evergreens and flowers, but the piece is so short that it would not be worth the while to do much in this way. So with costumes. *Flowers, grasses, wreaths* (green or autumn leaves, according to season), *holly berries, baskets of fruit,* &c., may be used by the singers according to their part, on their dresses, or in their hands.

---

* From George F. Root's "First Years in Song Land," by permission of the publishers, John Church & Co., Cincinnati. It can be used as a recitation, but will be far better with the music.

Old Year might have a long gray garment, a long white beard, and a faded crown; *New Year,* brighter garments and a new crown. *Winter* could have a dark garment, with cotton wool for snow-flakes, and alum crystals for frost. He wears a low crown; while *Spring, Summer,* and *Autumn* wear wreaths. The solo singers join in chorus after they get upon the stage.]

Old Year. AH, well! ah, well! I sadly tell!
My moments fleet are flying!
Like distant chime of Christmas bell,
The Old Year's hours are dying!

Good night, good night! good-by, good-by!
My long, bright reign is ending;
I see glad New Year drawing nigh,
My happy throne ascending.

New Year. I come, I come! I haste along,
The throne, the sceptre taking!
Appear, O loyal subject throng,
Your choice of service making.

Come, Autumn, Winter, Summer, Spring,
With wondrous varied graces;
And round the sun the earth we'll bring,
Along the starry spaces.

The Seasons (entering).
We come, we come!
Each Season brings her duty;
We'll crown the lovely earth, our home,
With joy and light and beauty.

Spring.   The Spring! the joyous Spring am I!
My handmaids see me bringing
Capricious April, wilful March,
And May with music ringing.

March.   The driving storm, the rushing gale,
Because you need, I send you,
But clear blue gleams, o'er hill and vale,
Through rifted clouds I lend you.

April.   You find the grass, the buds, the leaves,
Where through the shower I fling them,

And swallows build beneath the eaves,
   When home again I bring them.

May. And I, yes, I'm the merry May!
   The apple-trees are blooming,
And robin-redbreast's roundelay
   Sings out, to greet my coming.

March, April, May.
   Away, away!
   With all our gentle powers,
We break away the ice and snow,
   And strew the earth with flowers.

Summer. Away, bright Spring! my maids I bring,
   And each a welcome comer.
The brook shall laugh, the valleys sing,
   To greet the sunny Summer.

June. With daisies decked, with roses crowned,
   I bring the wild bee's humming,
And callow nestlings chirp around,
   When gentle June is coming.

July. Before me, glowing bright July,
   Flies every cloud and shadow,
While brilliant flowers, of deepest dye,
   I spread o'er hill and meadow.

August. And I dance o'er the sunny plain,
   A wealth of harvest finding,
Where merry reapers reap the grain
   That merry maids are binding.

June, July, August.
   We come, we come!
   At sunset hear them singing,
While o'er the new-mown fields they roam,
   And " Harvest-home " is ringing.

Autumn. Sweet Summer, haste! for on I fly
   To hang my golden treasure
On branches low, and branches high,
   Bright Autumn's fullest measure.

September. I crowd with fruits the tree, the vine,
And glad young hearts remember,
The Autumn leaves, that glow and shine
O'er joyous, gay September.

October. And I, in forests gay no more,
From woodlands brown and sober,
Shake down of nuts the children's store,
In frosty, keen October.

November. I wear no roses on my brow,
But Autumn leaflets growing,
And chill November, soft and low,
Sings, "Autumn-time is going."

September, October, November.
'Tis o'er, 'tis o'er !
The harvest merry-making,
And from the golden Autumn days
Our leave we now are taking.

Winter. My crown of ice, my robe of snow,
My frosty sandals wearing,
Before my brave young troop I go,
An icy sceptre bearing.

December. See gay December drawing near !
Glad Christmas I am bringing,
With Christmas gift, and song and cheer,
And merry bells a-ringing.

January. With sleigh-bells chime, and coasters' glee,
And skaters' shout, so merry,
Glad New Year smiles to welcome me,
His own bright January.

February. Last come I, changeful month that stands
'Twixt Winter's binding powers
And Spring, bright maid, whose tender hands
Sets free the buds and flowers.

Dec., Jan., Feb. Rejoice, rejoice ! in tuneful song
Raise all our happy voices,
The Months and Seasons haste along,
And every heart rejoices !

All. Rejoice, rejoice! again rejoice!
    He reigns in beauty o'er us;
    We greet the New Year on his throne,
      With full resounding chorus!

    He reigns, he reigns!
    He reigns in beauty o'er us!
    We greet the New Year on his throne,
      With full resounding chorus!

LINCOLN SONG: FOR APRIL 14TH.

(*Tune*: "Tenting on the old camp ground.")

WE are thinking to-day of a loved one lost,
    Lincoln, the true, the brave;
Of the strong one who came, when tempest-tost,
    Our nation's bark to save.

Chorus.   Many are the hearts that are mourning to-day,
      Mourning for the brave laid low;
    Many are the eyes looking up to say,
      Oh why must this be so!
    Help us to say, humbly we pray,
      Father, may thy will be done!

We are thinking to-day how he led us on,
    Just as the Lord led him,
To the glorious victory well-nigh won;
    And our eyes with tears grow dim.

Chorus.   Many are the hearts &c.

We are weeping to-day, but the hour will come,
    Come when we all shall see
Why the will of the Lord hath called him home,
    No more with us to be.

Chorus.   Many are the hearts, &c.

NO! NO! NO!*

THERE is a word of power
　　More strong than might of kings,
When, in temptation's hour,
　　Upon the ear it rings.
A thousand wiles would win us
　　In wicked ways to go,
Unless the voice within us
　　Tells us, No! No! No!

In gayest scenes of pleasure,
　　The wine-cup, gleaming bright,
May offer fullest measure
　　Of gladness and delight:
But oh, it lures to win us
　　Where bitter waters flow,
Unless the voice within us
　　Tells us, No! No! No!

In idle pastures straying
　　From labor's fields afar,
So easy is the staying,
　　So hard those duties are, —
The flowery paths would win us
　　Still more astray to go,
Unless the voice within us
　　Tells us, No! No! No!

There is a path of Duty,
　　There is a way of Right,
All full of truth and beauty,
　　Of honor, pure and bright.
Whatever thence would win us
　　Some other way to know,
Shall hear the voice within us
　　Tell us, No! No! No!

---

* This song is from W. O. Perkins's song-book, "The Whip-poor-will." "The Whip-poor-will" has songs for all the times and seasons, and occasions and needs of school life.

A LITTLE BOY'S SUGGESTION.

I DO not know one single thing
　About this Chinese question,
But I have thought that I would bring,
　To-night, this small suggestion :

'Tis just as true as 'twas when Christ
　This rule gave first and new,
That you must do to others as
　You'd have them do to you.

Now, do you think, if you should go
　To China or Japan,
You'd like such treatment as we give
　To poor John Chinaman ?

AUGUST, 1619. — DECEMBER, 1620.*

(Recitation for Forefathers' Day.)

'Twas a stormy night, and the moon's pale light
　Through rifted clouds shone down,
Where the Mayflower lay, in the ice-bound bay,
　By the rude, wild shore alone.
For a Pilgrim band to the northern land
　Had crossed the ocean o'er,
And a hope shone high in the lifted eye,
　As they gazed on the stormy shore.
　　What sought they, thus roaming
　　Far, far away?
Oh, they sought and found, where the soul, unbound,
　To the God of the free might pray !

To a southern clime, in the summer time,
　A barque ploughed through the sea ;
She was laden low with a freight of woe, —
　For a slaver ship was she.

---

* The Mayflower brought the Pilgrims to Plymouth, Mass., in December, 1620. In August of the preceding year, a Dutch slave-ship sailed up the James River with the first cargo of slaves ever brought to the American colonies.

O'er the sunny seas came a wooing breeze,
From fair Virginia's shore,
And the ship sailed in with her freight of sin,
And the blight and the curse she bore.
What brought she, thus roaming
Far o'er the sea?
Oh, she brought the slave, and the bondman gave
To the land of the Lord's own free!

O'er the northern hills, by the singing rills,
From the mountains to the sea,
Spread a mighty throng, brave and true and strong,
And they sang the songs of the free.
While Virginia's soil with the bondman's toil,
Fair as a garden grew;
Till Jehovah's breath with a blast of death
O'er the sin-cursed nation blew!
What sought He, Jehovah,
Lord over all?
Oh, he brought out free, through the War's Red Sea,
His oppressed from Oppression's thrall.

"ALL WORK AND NO PLAY."

(*Said two ways.*)

Little Boy (thoughtfully).
IT does *not* seem to me that boys
Get half the fun they need,
When they just come to school, and learn
To write, and spell, and read.

But then, it does *not* seem to me
That it is just the way
For boys to skate, and slide, and run,
And spend all time in play.

Small Girl (interrupting briskly).
That's *just* the way our fathers thought,
Full fifty years ago!
This is the way they said it,
Not musingly and slow:
" All work and no play makes Jack a dull boy.
All play and no work makes Jack a mere toy."

VACATION FUN.

[Some *Boys* and *Girls* are talking together. *Little Grandmother* sits
   off at one side, knitting, and commenting in an aside as they speak,
   but not interrupting them.]

Archie.   Boys and girls, vacation is coming,
    And now let's all of us say
    Where we would go, and what we would see,
    If things could be as they ought to be,
    And boys and girls had their own way.

Grandmother.
    " Had their own way ! "   'Tis my belief
    In a very short time they'd come to grief.

Shelton.   Oh, Archie ! I wouldn't take long to decide :
    I'd build a beautiful boat ;
    To the Northern Polar Sea I'd sail,
    And catch the walrus, and seal, and whale,
    And that would be fun afloat !

Grand.   In his beautiful boat he'd have a mess
    With walrus, and seal, and whale, I guess.

Ethel.   Now, Shelton, I'd choose something better than that :
    Up the Amazon I'd run,
    Where parrots chatter, and monkeys swing,
    And bright little humming-birds flit and sing, —
    And oh, wouldn't that be fun !

Grand.   Now hear the child talk !   It makes me smile.
    Nice dinner she'd make for a crocodile !

Gerty.   Oh, Ethel ! see how you like my plan : —
    I'll have a seal-skin dress,
    Then up to the Hudson's Bay I'll go
    To the queer snow-huts of the Esquimaux,
    And that will be fun, I guess !

Grand.   Has that girl forgotten, do you suppose,
    It is cold enough there to freeze her nose ?

Lulu. I can tell you a trip worth two of that,
   Nor half so cold and rough ;
   For a girl of my studious disposition,
   In a trip to the Paris Exposition
   Of fun there would be enough. .

Grand. Poor thing ! half frightened to death she'd be
   Before she was half-way over the sea !

Robbie. Now, Lulu, to China, the land of tea,
   I make up my mind to go ;
   Where they have such queer little slanting eyes,
   And sell young rats and puppies for pies, —
   And that must be fun, you know !

Grand. (*turning to them*).
   Well ! well ! it seems you would each forsake
   The land I jolliest call.
   Better sail your boats in the Yankee rills ;
   Better chase for sport over Yankee hills ;
   That will be the best fun of all.

All. Little grandmother's right ! Three cheers for you !
   Your way is the wisest one.
   Wherever we go, she shall lead the van,
   She shall march this way, — now see our plan, —
   And isn't this jolly fun !
   Yes, isn't this jolly fun !

(*Two Boys take* LITTLE GRANDMOTHER *between them, in her little arm-chair, and carry her off the stage, the rest following.*)

MONEY TO SPEND.

(*Game for Rainy Recess.*)

(*The Scholars sit in a line or semicircle. Each Scholar takes the name of a country.*)

The Leader (*standing before them, addressing any one*). I have money to spend : what have you to sell (*turning quickly to Spain*), Mr. Spain?

Spain (*instantly*). Malaga raisins, sir.

Spain (having answered promptly, takes the Leader's place, and says), I have money to spend : what have you to sell, Mr. Labrador?

Labrador (hesitates, and cannot tell).

Leader. Go to your storehouse and find out. (*A Labrador leans his head upon his hands until he can remember, when he raises a hand, is called upon, and tells.*)

Leader. I have money to spend : what have you to sell, Florida?

Florida. Oranges, sir. (*And Florida takes the lead.*)

[The variety of heads down, hands up, and changing places, is amusing. Vary thus :]

Leader. I am collector for a menagerie : what animal have you, Alaska?

Alaska. Seals, sir.

[Or again :]

Leader. I am seeking for wonders : what have you, Iceland?

Iceland. My geysers, sir.

[This game, briskly carried on, is amusing and instructive.]

WHAT SHALL ARCHIE DO?

Q. WHAT shall Archie do
  In the month of the glad New Year?

A. Slide down hill with his splendid sled,
  And skate on the ice so clear.

Q. And what shall Archie do
  In the month that will soonest end?

A. Paint pretty things on pretty cards,
  To his Valentine to send.

Q. And what shall Archie do
  When the winds of March rage wild?

A. Put on his ulster, tie his hat,
  And run like a happy child.

Q. And what shall Archie do
  In the changing April days?

A. Watch the swift raindrops patter down,
  In their pretty dancing plays.

Q. And what shall Archie do
    When May is bright and fair ?

A. Wander over to yonder hill,
    And find blue violets there.

Q. And what shall Archie do
    When comes the rosy June ?

A. Lie on the still, soft grass, and hear
    The insects' busy tune.

Q. And what shall Archie do
    When comes the warm July ?

A. Celebrate the glorious Fourth,
    And send his rockets high.

Q. And what shall Archie do
    In August, hotter still ?

A. Swing in his hammock under the trees,
    And listen to Oriole's trill.

Q. And what shall Archie do
    In the bright September weather ?

A. He and I will fish in the brook,
    Or pick up the nuts together.

Q. And what shall Archie do
    When October days come cool ?

A. Watch the wild geese as they fly off south,
    By their queer, triangular rule.

Q. And what shall Archie do
    In the next month, tell me, pray ?

A. Go to grandmother's, for you know
    In November's Thanksgiving day.

Q. And what shall Archie do
    In December, bleak and cold ?

A. Give poor little children gifts, and find
    For himself more than stockings can hold.

But all this while must Archie
  This lesson, too, remember : —
Time is not given all for play,
  From New Year to December ;
And all this time he must learn
  From Nature and books all he can,
That will help him to be what he's made to be,
  A thoroughly noble man.

SPRING FUN.

THE best of fun, I tell you, boys, —
  I wonder if you know ? —
Is to get a dozen polliwigs,
  And find out how frogs grow.

You go and catch them in the pond,
  Along in early spring ;
And when you stir them up, — oh, my !
  They squirm like anything.

They are just like a little spot
  Of jelly, with two eyes ;
And such a very funny tail,
  Of quite astounding size.

You put them in a great, big dish, —
  A large bowl is the best, —
They swim and squirm, and squirm and swim,
  And never seem to rest.

Put in some dirt, and water-plants, —
  I've known them to eat meat, —
They'll grow and grow so beautiful,
  The *girls* would call them " *sweet.*"

And bunches, by and by, appear, —
  On each side there are two, —
And little legs, like sprouting plants,
  Will pretty soon peep through.

The legs grow long, the tail grows short,
  And by and by you'll see
8

There isn't any tail at all
Where a tail used to be.

And froggy now can jump on land,
Or in the water swim ;
And scientific men will now
Amphibious call him.

TWO MITES : A LITTLE MISUNDERSTANDING.

SUCH a funny thing is told to me,
And now I tell to you,
What a child as poor as poor can be,
For the missions tried to do.

The story of the widow's *mite*
Had taught this lesson, good :
Each gift is blessed in the dear Lord's sight
When we have done what we could.

Next Sabbath day said the little child,
" I've dot *two mice* for you."
" Two mice ! " the teacher said, and smiled ;
" What with them can I do ? "

" I've brought my own two mice," she said,
" My *tontybution*, these ;
You said, you know, that with *two mice*
The dear Lord once was pleased ! "

Hushed was the rising merriment ;
The two mice soon were sold ;
Freely for them the rich ones spent
Their silver and their gold.

Ah ! how they raised and raised the price,
All for the mission store !
So big a price for two small mice
Was never paid before !

Thus, sure enough, the gift was blessed,
The giver's heart made glad ;
And so grew " more than all the rest,"
That poor child's " all she had " !

A LITTLE FRENCH FOR A LITTLE GIRL.

" ' EARLY to bed and early to rise.'
So, little girlie, come shut up your eyes."

" *Mes yeux,* that's my eyes, will not shut up, *mon père,*
Because the old sandman has not been round there."

Mon père is my father, and this, *couchez-vous,*
Just means, go to bed, as papa calls to you.

A huit heures, eight o'clock, should you linger, he'd say,
" *Ma fille,* that's my daughter, *il vous faut aller.*"

" You must go ; " so, my darling, come give me a kiss,
These French words, *embrasse moi,* mean just about this.

So, my girlie, go off with your mother, *ta mère.*
Who will carefully comb *tes cheveux,* that's your hair.

She will lovingly kiss you, and say *bon nuit,*
Or good-night, and in dreamland you quickly will be.

MOUSE–TRAPS.*

SAY, did you ever a mouse-trap behold,
Framed to entrap all the silly young mice ;
Tempting them, luring them on to be bold ; —
Sweetest of morsels within to entice?
Did not you think, if a mousie were you,
You would know better than nibbling to go?
Then, if *you're* tempted some wrong thing to do,
Just think of the mouse-trap, and wisely say *No !*

Chorus. Mouse-traps ! mouse-traps ! beware !
Mouse-traps ! of these have a care !
Temptation shun, and say, when you see
Sly, cunning mouse-traps, You shall not catch me !

Say, did you ever a mouse-trap behold,
When it had snapped on some poor, little mouse, —
Holding him, keeping him there in the cold,
Shutting him up in a dark prison-house?

---

* Use as a Recitation, omitting the Chorus; or find music in
" Golden Robin," published by Oliver Ditson, Boston.

Did not you think, though the morsels were nice,
  Better with crusts and with freedom to go?
Then, if the wicked try *you* to entice,
  Just think of the mouse-trap, and wisely say *No!*

Chorus. Mouse-traps! mouse-traps! beware!

Say, did you ever a mouse-trap behold;
  Little brown mouse lying dead on the floor?
Did not you wish that somebody had told
  Mousie to seek other quarters before?
Surely, the way of trangressors is hard:
  Always remember, my boys, *it is so!*
All of the wiles of the tempter discard;
  Just think of the mouse-trap, and wisely say *No!*

Chorus. Mouse-traps! mouse-traps! beware!

WE THANK THEE.

(*For Opening School.*)

(*Let five Girls recite each a single stanza, and the whole school
respond, reverently, in concert.*)

First.   FOR flowers that bloom about our feet,
      For tender grass, so fresh, so sweet,
      For song of bird, and hum of bee,
      For all things fair we hear or see, —

Response.   Father in heaven, we thank Thee!

Second. For blue of stream and blue of sky,
      For pleasant shade of branches high,
      For fragrant air and cooling breeze,
      For beauty of the blooming trees, —

Response.   Father in heaven, we thank Thee!

Third.   For mother-love and father-care,
      For brothers strong and sisters fair,
      For love at home and school each day,
      For guidance lest we go astray, —

Response.   Father in heaven, we thank Thee!

Fourth.	For Thy dear everlasting arms That bear us o'er all ills and harms, For blessed words of long ago That help us now Thy will to know, —
Response.	Father in heaven, we thank Thee!
Fifth.	We bring to crown the children's hour The season's wealth of leaf and flower, And from our loving hearts we say, For Summer-time and *Children's day,*
Response.	Father in heaven, we thank Thee!

LITTLE FOXES AND LITTLE HUNTERS.

Recite. "Take us the foxes, the little foxes, that spoil the vines." — SONG OF SOLOMON, II. 15.

First.	AMONG my tender vines I spy A little fox named — *By-and-by.*
Answer.	Then set upon him, quick, I say, The swift young hunter — *Right-away.*
Second.	Around each tender vine I plant, I find the little fox — *I-can't.*
Answer.	Then, fast as ever hunter ran, Chase him with bold and brave — *I-can!*
Third.	*No-use-in-trying* — lags and whines This fox, among my tender vines.
Answer.	Then drive him low and drive him high, With this good hunter named — *I'll-try!*
Fourth.	Among the vines in my small lot, Creeps in the young fox — *I-forgot.*
Answer.	Then hunt him out and to his den With — *I-will-not-forget-again!*

Fifth.	The little fox that, hidden there Among my vines is — *I-don't-care.*
Answer.	Then let *I'm-sorry* — hunter true — Chase him a-far from vines and you.
The Five.	What mischief-making foxes! yet Among our vines they often get.
In concert.	But, now their hunters' names you know, Just drive them out, *and keep them so.*

CALL TO THE BIRDS.

COME, come, come!
Birdlings, hasten home.
Spring has called the buds and flowers,
Clad with green the wildwood bowers;
Bees begin to hum,
Happy birdlings, come.

Fly, fly, fly!
Through the pleasant sky.
Fly from sunny southern meadows;
Fly as swift as Summer shadows,
Summer time draws nigh,
Happy birdlings, fly.

Sing, sing, sing!
On the waving wing.
Sing aloud in tuneful chorus;
Sing your sweetest songs before us.
Making glad the Spring,
Happy birdlings, sing.

Build, build, build!
Nests must soon be filled.
Here a straw and there a feather,
Neatly woven, all together.
Sunshine comes to gild,
Happy birdlings, build.

Haste, haste, haste!
O'er the ocean waste.
He who heeds the sparrow's falling
Guides you when the spring is calling.
He your path has traced,
Happy birdlings, haste.

THE CITY GIRL.

Up in the morning early,
  Roused by the rush of feet,
Hurrying over the pavements,
  Hastening down the street.
Called by the school-bell merry,
  Joining the scholars' play,
Seeing the sights so cheery,
  Filling the windows gay.

Watching the rich man's horses,
  Bearing him swift along ;
Watching the man with an organ,
  The little girl singing a song ;
Seeing, — ah ! many a lady,
  Decked like a splendid queen ;
Seeing, — ah! many a beggar,
  Covered with garments mean ;

Pausing to hear the church-bells
  Ringing in solemn chime ;
Pausing to count, from the belfry,
  The hour of the passing time.
Thus, to the child in the city
  Life goes hurrying by,
Happy the one that treasures
  The minutes that swiftly fly.

Oh ! may we, all of us, ever
  Pause in our heedless haste,
By the fountain that fails us never,
  The waters of life to taste.
So, when life's labors are ended,
  Joyfully we may meet
Up in the *Heavenly City,*
  Walking the Golden Street.

LUCY LEE.

DOWN the hill, down the hill, where the lilies grow,
Where the willow-branches droop, and where the waters flow,
Dwelt a little friend of ours, sweet little Lucy Lee ;
No purer were the lily flowers beneath the willow-tree.
Down the hill, down the hill, where the lilies grow,
Where the willow-branches droop, and where the waters flow.

On the hill, on the hill, joyfully and free,
Through the livelong summer day, played little Lucy Lee,
But when Autumn tinged the trees that grow beside the wave,
They bore our darling one away to yonder little grave ;
Then no more upon the hill, joyfully and free,
Through the livelong summer day played little Lucy Lee.

O'er the hill, o'er the hill, solemnly and slow,
Carried they our little friend, to yonder church-yard low ;
They laid the little Lucy down within her lowly grave,
And all the lilies faded, too, that grew beside the wave.
O'er the hill, o'er the hill, solemnly and slow,
Carried they our little friend to yonder church-yard low.

Up the hill! up the hill, gentle angels bore
The lovely one that we shall see upon the earth no more.
For only Lucy's body, then, to yonder grave was given ;
Her happy spirit plays again, upon the Hills of Heaven !
Up the hill! up the hill, gentle angels bore
The lovely one that we shall see upon the earth no more.

HAPPY SINGER.

THE Spring has come with happy hours ;
  The sun shines all the day.
I love to see the blooming flowers
  Beneath the skies of May.
But better than the flowers I see,
  I love the birds that sing ;
For music dearer is to me
  Than any other thing.

In Summer time the roses blow
  Upon the sunny hills;
The lilies and the daises grow
  Beside the singing rills.
But better than the flowers I see,
  I love the brooks that sing;
For music dearer is to me
  Than any other thing.

Though Spring and Summer fly away,
  And hushed each singing rill, —
Though not a bird in all the day
  Sings o'er the silent hill, —
My happy heart, so full of glee,
  Its merry song shall sing;
For music dearer is to me
  Than any other thing.

THE CHRISTMAS-TREE.

DEEP in the greenwood, tall and strong,
The grand old oak-tree standeth long.

The cypress shadeth the precious grave;
And the willow bendeth beside the wave.

The apple-trees sweeten the summer air,
The holly and pine make winter fair.

And many another beautiful tree,
Over the hills and vales you see.

But one that giveth a new delight,
Shall bud and blossom for us to-night;

Its leaves are green and the trunk is strong;
There are curious fruits its boughs among.

'Tis the Christmas-tree, and soon you'll know
The wonderful fruits that on it grow:

Here are mantles, and aprons, and gloves, and mittens,
And wooden houses, and sugar kittens ;

And books with pictures, and books without ;
I wish I knew what they're all about !

There are dolls and trumpets, for girls and boys ;
And useful clothing, and pretty toys ;

And every leaf and twig that you see,
Is as dewy with love as a twig can be.

And now, dear children, its fruits so fair,
We'll gather, and give to each his share.

But, no matter who plants a tree, you know
It is only our Lord that can make it grow.

And so, dear children, your hearts uplift
To the Author of every perfect gift.

And for all the fruits of the Christmas-tree,
Though the loving givers around you see,

Be sure your thanks alike shall rise,
To the dear, kind Father above the skies.

BIRDS AND ANGELS.

ONE day in early Spring,
　My little girls and boys,
Each merry-hearted thing
　Seemed bent on making noise.

" Oh, listen now," said I,
　" Who knows but we may hear
Up in the branches high,
　Some Spring-bird's voice so clear ! "

Quickly each little child
    Ceased from his busy play,
And waited, still and mild,
    For what the bird should say.

And sweet, and clear, and long,
    The little listeners heard
The merry, happy song
    Of a little bright Spring bird.

And thus, so glad and gay,
    That joyful little thing
Had sung for us all day,
    And we ne'er listening!

How could we, when the din
    Of noise and tumult round
Would never let come in
    The sweeter, better sound?

Then thought I how the angels
    Are near us night and day,
Though evil passions sometimes
    Would drive them far away.

No wonder that we never
    Their sweet, low voices hear,
If round our lives forever
    We keep confusion near!

Just like good little children
    Let us, obedient, stay
Of sin the noise and tumult,
    And hear *what angels say.*

For, like the birds unheeded,
    With songs as sweet and fair,
The good and blessed angels
    Are near us everywhere.

MAY FESTIVAL.

1. [Entrance of the *Queen*, the three *Maids of Honor*, and three *Pages* bearing the *Garland*, *Crown*, and *Sceptre*. Then follow all the other children. After marching around the stage, the *Queen* with the *Maids of Honor* and *Pages* take position at the front of the stage : *Queen* in the centre, *Maids of Honor* on the right, *Pages* on the left. The others stand in groups on either side.]

2. PRESENTATION OF THE GARLAND.

A *Little Boy* steps forward, takes the *Garland* from the *First Page*, who has previously carried it, and throws it over the *Queen's* shoulder, after reciting the following presentation speech :

> THOU art the Queen of May.
> As May throws over the land
> Bright garlands of beauty,
> My loyal duty
> Is thus with loving hand
> To fling this Garland green
> Over the neck of our Queen.

Queen (replies after receiving Garland).

> For thy loyal hand to deck,
> Low I bend my royal neck.
> Lovely is this garland gay,
> That adorns your Queen of May.

3. PRESENTATION OF THE CROWN.

(Another Little Boy steps forward, takes the Crown from the Second Page and places it on the Queen's head, saying:)

> Spring is queen of the year,
> And May is queen of the Spring ;
> Thou art the Queen of the May, most dear,
> And so thy crown I bring.
> Bend thy beautiful head, I pray,
> That I may crown thee Queen of May.

Queen (receiving Crown).

> Brighter far than gold or gem,
> I this flowery diadem
> Wear, upon my brow, to-day,
> That shall crown your Queen of May.

(*After the crowning, all sing the first stanza of* "The Rosy Crown," *or of any familiar crowning song.*)

4. Presentation of the Sceptre.

(*A third Little Boy takes the Sceptre from the Third Page, presents it, and recites:*)

Gentle is thy royal mien ;
Rule as gently, lovely Queen.
Now thy flowery sceptre hold,
Bright with gems of green and gold.

Queen (receiving Sceptre).

Sceptre, bright with leaf and flower, —
Token of my queenly power, —
Love shall guide its royal sway
While I rule as Queen of May.

[After the *Queen* has responded, she and the *Maids of Honor*, and *Pages*, walk to the Throne and take seats there.]

5. Grand March.

[After which all the children form a semicircle around the Throne.]

6. Call to the Flowers.

[A *Young Lady* steps to the front of the stage and sings the Call. At the close of each verse, the Flower called steps to the side of the singer, recites a little verse, and then takes her seat at the foot of the Throne near the feet of the *Queen*.]

Young Lady.

Now bloom the bright buttercups, golden-hued buttercups,
  Down in the meadow-grass green ;
Come, come, little Buttercup, bright little Buttercup,
  Bloom round the throne of our Queen.

Buttercup.   Yes, I'm coming ; help me up ;
    I am little Buttercup.
              (*These responses are recited.*)

Young Lady.

Sweet roses are blossoming, blushing and blossoming ;
  Down from the branches they lean ;
Come, come, little Rosy-bud, sweet little Rosy-bud,
  Bloom round the throne of our Queen.

Rosebud.   Yes, I'm coming to her feet;
              I'm a little Rosebud sweet.

Young Lady.
And modest blue violets, sweet-scented violets,
    Down by the brooklet are seen;
Come, come, little Violet, meek little Violet,
    Bloom round the throne of our Queen.

Violet.   Yes, I'm coming very nigh;
             Little Violet am I.

Young Lady.
Now beautiful May-flowers, loveliest May-flowers,
    Hide under brown leaves their sheen;
Come, come, little May-flower, sweet little May-flower,
    Bloom round the throne of our Queen.

May-flower. Yes, I'm coming; lead me there;
              I'm the little May-flower fair.

Young Lady.
And daisies white, daisies white, bloom in the meadows bright,
    Modest and simple their mien;
Come, come, little Daisy-white, dear little Daisy-white,
    Bloom round the throne of our Queen.

Daisy.   Yes, I'm Daisy, white as snow;
             To my Queen I'm glad to go.

Young Lady.
Now with their bright glancing wings, happy and dancing things,
    Butterflies golden are seen;
Come, come, little Butterflies, gay little Butterflies,
    Flit round the throne of your Queen.

Butterfly. Yes, I'm coming; gay am I;
              I'm the golden Butterfly.

[All these Little Ones should be dressed in the appropriate colors and
    flowers. There may be two of each kind if desirable. Of the "But-
    terflies" it would be pretty to have several. Make butterfly-wings
    of yellow tarlatan, over a wire frame, butterfly-wing shape.]

7. ENTRANCE OF THE QUEEN'S GUARD.

[A band of the very smallest Boys enter. They march to front of
stage, and stand in line. Each has a shield on his left arm, and a
spear in right hand.]

(*The Leader says one line, and the others in concert reply.*)

Leader. I am the Captain of the May Queen's Band.

All. And we are the Band.

Leader. I hold my Lance in my hand, you see.

All. And so do we.

Leader. For our good Queen brave deeds I'll do.

All. And we will, too.

Leader. For our good Queen now shout Hurrah!

All. Hurrah! hurrah!

(*Then let them march around the stage, and take places near
the Throne.*)

[Or use these lines instead.]

Leader. I am the Captain of the May Queen's Guard;
If anybody harms her I shall fight him hard.

All. And so shall we!

Leader. And that no danger shall come upon her,
I pledge my life and my sacred honor!

All. And so do we!

Leader. And now I bravely take my stand —
The May Queen's Guard at the Queen's right hand.

All. And so do we.

(*Then let them march around and take places by the Throne.
Hold the Lances and Shields in some pretty way as they
recite.*)

Leader. Beloved Queen! if enemies assail her,
Or harm affect her, —

All. We promise her that we will *never* fail her!
We will *protect* her!

Leader. Beloved Queen! should danger come upon her,
Or foes come nigh her, —

All. We pledge our lives, we pledge our sacred honor,
That we'll stand by her!

[The *Queen's Guard* now march to the *Throne*, half standing on the right, and half on the left. A *Young Lady* sings to "We sail the ocean blue," the opening chorus in "Pinafore."]

Our lovely Queen we've crowned,
She's the Queen of May and beauty;
We stand her throne around,
And we pledge our loyal duty.
We have called to her feet every bright Flower sweet,
For her we will dance and sing;
And our May-pole we'll braid for the lovely maid,
For she rules o'er the May-pole ring.

8. The *Twelve Girls* who take part in the May-pole Dance, now

BRAID THE MAY-POLE.

a. Twining and untwining.
b. Singing the second verse of "Rosy Crown."
c. Braiding and unbraiding.
d. Third verse of "Rosy Crown."

While singing the last Chorus, the *Twelve Little Girls* join hands and dance once or twice around the Pole.

THE BRAIDING OF THE MAY-POLE.

[Let the pole be as high as the room will admit. It is decorated with showy wreath at top. There are twelve ribbons: four red, four white, and four blue. These are all tacked to the top of the pole, and must be long enough to reach to the bottom of the pole. They must hang perfectly smooth and even. The Twelve who are to braid the May-pole are in two circles, an inner and an outer. The music is any simple polka. Each circle has a leader; one goes to the right, one to the left. This braiding the May-pole is beautiful, but it requires a great deal of practice. Use, in practising, long strips of colored cloth instead of ribbons. After braiding the pole, the Twelve fall again into the general line; all join hands, and dance around in a circle; at a certain point the Queen and Attendants descend, and all march in pretty figures in and out and off the stage.]

SWEET CLOVER STORIES.

HENRY A. YOUNG & CO.

EARL WHITING;

OR,

THE NAMELESS BOY.

By the author of THE LITTLE PEANUT MERCHANT.

1 Vol. 16mo. - - - - Price $1.75.

Elegantly bound in black and gilt.

"It is of a high moral and intellectual tone, and is a safe book to be put into the hands of our boys and girls."

PUBLISHED BY

HENRY A. YOUNG & CO., Boston, Mass.

Happy Home Stories.

By the author of AUNT HATTIE'S LIBRARY.

6 vols. 18mo . . . . . Price $3.00.

Diligent Dick.   Little Fritz.
Cousin Willie.   Bertie and his Sisters.
Lazy Robert.   The New Buggy.

This is an entirely new series for boys, by this popular author.
A new series for girls will be ready early in the fall.

Published by

HENRY A. YOUNG & CO., Boston, Mass.

SYLVAN GLEN SERIES.

4 vols. 16mo. Price $5.00.

Elegantly bound in black and gilt.

Jamie Noble.
Out of Wilderness.
Breaking the Rules.
Deeds Louder than Words.

A beautiful set of books for boys or girls.

Published by

HENRY A. YOUNG & CO., Boston, Mass.

GOLDEN MOTTO SERIES.

4 Vols. 16mo. - - - Price $5.00.

Elegantly bound in black and gilt.

Golden Motto,
Young Adventurer,
True Friendships,
Runaway Boy.

Very interesting and attractive books for the young.

PUBLISHED BY
HENRY A. YOUNG & CO., Boston, Mass.

THE HERMIT OF HOLCOMBE.

By MARY DWINELL CHELLIS.

1 Vol. 16mo.   -   -   -   -   Price $1.50.

This is the Fourth and concluding volume of the

Standard Series of Temperance Tales.

No better books on Temperance than these have been written.

Published by

HENRY A. YOUNG & CO.,
Boston, Mass.

Books for the Little Ones.

SWEET-BRIER STORIES.

CHARLEY'S LOCKET.
YOUNG BIRD-CATCHERS.
THE PICTURE CLOCK,
WILL AND THE DONKEY.
WOOLLY BEAR.
WILFUL WALTER.

LITTLE MAGGIE.
THE PET SPARROW.
SUSIE'S VICTORY.
SIX MINCE PIES.
RIPE STRAWBERRIES.
SILK APRON.

12 vols., 32mo. In neat box, $3.00.

MOSS-ROSE SERIES.

WILLIE'S WISH.
CURIOUS TOM.
THE TWO MOTTOES.
LITTLE JAMES.
OLD BEN'S STOCKINGS.
LITTLE BERTIE.

AFRAID OF THE DARK.
LITTLE MINNIE.
BIRTHDAY PRESENT.
A REAL VICTORY.
SOWING LITTLE SEEDS.
MILLY'S DOVES.

12 vols., 32mo. Handsomely Illustrated, $3.00.

LITTLE FAVORITES' LIBRARY.

HIDE AND SEEK.
TWO RULES.
LITTLE CONSCIENCE.
CLARENCE'S SECRET.
GOLDEN PENNIES.
STOLEN SHILLING.

JESSIE'S HOLIDAY.
LITTLE ANNIE.
MARY AND WILLIE.
MARION'S JEWELS.
EFFIE'S CHRISTMAS.
TWO SISTERS.

12 vols., 32mo. $3.00.

PICTURE-STORIES FOR LITTLE FOLKS.
VIZ.:

LITTLE STORIES FOR LITTLE PEOPLE.
SCENES IN THE CITY AND COUNTRY.
RHYMES AND STORIES FOR LITTLE FOLKS.
FRANK'S PET ROOSTER, AND OTHER STORIES.
THE WHITE SWAN, AND OTHER STORIES.
PICTURE STORIES FOR LITTLE FOLKS.

6 vols., 32mo. $1.50.

www.ingramcontent.com/pod-product-compliance
Lightning Source LLC
Chambersburg PA
CBHW030607270326
41927CB00007B/1088